Table of Contents

Dedicated to my parents and sisters

ACKNOWLEDGEMENT

With God's grace and the blessings of my parents and sisters, I would like mention of few people who played a key role in my professional career. I would like to take this opportunity to thank Utkarsh(bhai) Patel, Samir Chokshi, Tracy Abdo, and Rick Wilhelm for their kind advice and support!

My deepest gratitude extends to my friends and colleagues who helped me and gave feedback while I was writing this book: Harry Lalor, Rick Wilhelm, and Dr. Satyam Priyadarshy.

I would also like to take the opportunity to mention Ratan Tata, Bill Gates, Steve Jobs, Warren Buffet, and Oprah Winfrey. Their work has always been an inspiration to me and they continue to inspire me in my work.

PREFACE

I often read or hear on the news about how we should all be smarter with our money. Especially in America, I hear a lot about how Americans are bad with money—failing to save smartly while racking up high credit and paying a lot of interest. Around April or May 2012, I was watching one such news story and decided that maybe I should try and do something about it. I have always strongly believed that my practical way of living led me to financial freedom and I thought I could pass this message along. Living well while saving wisely is something that is absolutely doable and something that should be a part of our lives. At the time that this idea came to me, I was not quite sure what I should do or how I should approach it. My thoughts became stronger and I decided that I could probably create a mobile app, a website, a blog, or a book (or all of the above!) to chronicle my experiences. After all these thoughts, I knew I had to look back and detail all my experiences that would make up the content of this production. I had to go back and really think about everything that led me to achieve financial freedom and the million dollar mark at end of December 2012. In doing so, I ended up with the book you hold in your hand—a history of the past 14 years of my life and how I got to be where I am today.

HOW IS THE BOOK ORGANIZED

Here is the layout of the book and what you can expect from this section:

- **Chapters:** I have laid out the chapters in form of years to show the flow of my gradual progress and challenges, year after year.

- **Events:** In each chapter, I have attempted to touch on my experiences and events that shaped my financial life.

- **Insightful Tips:** I have attempted to insert the most valuable and insightful tips that I learned from each life experience.

- **Financial Charts:** I demonstrate my financial journey in the form of charts at the end of each chapter to show and summarize everything I touched on in a graphical manner.

- **Spending and Investment Insights:** I also provide some insight into my spending habits and investment approach and how they evolved over the years.

SETTING THE STAGE

Before I get started on my journey of gaining financial freedom and achieving million dollar mark, I want to take few minutes describing some of the key points I hope you will pay attention to while reading this book:

- Audiences will learn the art of smart savings in their day-to-day life and live well.

- Learning the art of smart savings need not be interpreted as leading a miserly life, but it should instead be interpreted as living a wiser life.

- No one achieves financial freedom and becomes millionaire overnight—unless it is by winning the lottery! It takes time and good habits.

- Failure and de-motivation are a part of life, but the ones who keep moving past these obstacles are the true winners in the long run. When you start to lose motivation thinking about how much more you need to do, think back on how much you have already accomplished! Is it worth letting all that effort go to waste?

- It's never too late to start changing what is in your control.

- For couples who are both working and earning, they can save even more and achieve their goal of financial freedom even faster. With the right partner, it's always a big benefit!

- The 80-20 rule—also known as "the law of the vital few"—is a rule of thumb that states that 80% of outcomes can be attributed to 20% of the causes for a given event. This principle is a very powerful and effective tool that one can exercise in their life for

  * Smart Savings

  * Friends & social circles

  * Time management

  * Work

- Franchise model - My smart savings model is like a franchise-it can be recreated in different environments by sticking to the same basic structure. However, if you find it difficult or feel that it is causing more stress, you may need to tweak certain aspects to fit your life. Roots of my smart savings model go back to my early life learning from my parents.

- Above all, the key is to make the effort to start and find the drive to commit. This is what I like to call the "commit force"—this is beyond your passion, beyond a resolution, beyond your motivation to start. It is what will keep you moving towards your goal even when your goal is very far away. What is pushing you? What is forcing you to commit? Identify this factor and keep it in your sight even when your goal is not.

The amount of money you have has got nothing to do with what you earn. People earning a million dollars a year can have no money. People earning $35,000 a year can be quite well off. It's not what you earn, it's how you spend.

- Paul Clitheroe

PRIOR TO 1999

I was born in the beautiful city of Ahmedabad, Gujarat (known as the "Manchester of India") in 1974. I was born in a Punjabi family who was in the process of settling down in Gujarat after moving from North India. My father had moved to accept a new job in Gujarat at the age of 36 along with my mother and my eldest sister.

It is important for me to give some quick background about my family to show that almost every family in this world, no matter how rich or poor, goes through financial cycles in each generation. One should always be sensitive to these changes and never give up during the hardest times.

My father was born to a royal family in northern India. He was grandson to a Rao Bahadur. Rao Bahadur ("Rao" means "prince" and "Bahadur" means "brave" or "most honorable") was a title of honor issued with a medal to individuals who had performed a great service to the nation during British rule. It was awarded to both Hindu and Christian Indians. One could say it is the equivalent of the Order of British Empire (OBE).

I heard stories about my great grandfather during my early childhood from my parents, relatives, and friends of our family. I can say that my father's early childhood was nothing less than a royal prince life. He had the honor of riding around the streets of northern India on royal horse and elephant chariots owned by my great grandfather. At that time, we owned diversified businesses including cotton textile industries, sugar mills, timber forest contracts all across northern India, as well as major investments in the stock market. My great grandfather got his Rao Bahadur title because of his charitible activities (including donating to colleges and giving away acres of land). One might wonder that if my father had so much wealth, then what drove him to start his life from zero? This was the time of India's independence and the India-Pakistan Conflict. Right around the time when the fight for independence was at its peak, my great grandfather suffered a sudden death. His sudden death, the fighting, the India-Pakistan Partition, and the following riots resulted in a situation that stripped the family of the business, money, and property that had allowed them to live that luxurious life. My father's lifestyle was severely downgraded, leaving him to take on side jobs in order to continue his education.

In his early professional career, my father served in the Indian army. He left the armed services due to some family commitments. After leaving army at the age of 29, married my mother and they soon had my eldest sister. At this time, my father had been helping out with family business (an automobile workshop) and funneled most of his army savings into expanding this business. However, his attempts at expansion failed and caused a financial and emotional setback which led to some health issues. With a lot of motivation from my mother, my father fought back to regain his health and start from the very beginning. This time, my father started reaching out to companies who needed his skills and tried to land a permanent job. After few months, he managed to find the job in Gujarat. My parents travelled with two bags of clothes and utensils (their only real assets) and restarted their life from ground up. My father was 36 years old at this time. From here on, he tended to his life and finances wisely, allowing him to retire by the age of 58.

It is amazing to remember some of my childhood memories and only now I really understand how wisely my parents acted when it came to finances. When they were buying their first home, they had the option to purchase a bungalow (a single family home) with a higher mortgage, or a comparatively smaller model with a lower mortgage. Though it would have been nice to have the extra space, my parents realized that the smaller home would fit their needs just as well, and that they would be able to manage the mortgage payments easier. Aside from that, my father used to ride his bike to work instead of a motorbike or scooter, and my mother would opt to walk instead of taking the bus or the taxi. With these small decisions, they showed me a model of restraint and practicality. Even when it came to leisure, my parents chose activities that would be less expensive than say, going to the movies (which my dad loved to do). Instead, we took family picnics and went to nearby gardens and park. It is only now that I realize how some of their smartest saving decisions might have been small, but others were truly an act of sacrifice on their part. I can appreciate their motives for they allowed my sisters and me to experience a lot more financial freedom in our older years.

I remember on the weekends both of them would work on home improvement projects by themselves even though manual labor is relatively cheap in India. They could have hired contractors for building fences or painting the house or building a play area in the backyard, but chose to take such home improvement activities on themselves. My mother used to amaze all of us with her creativity and her interior decorating skills. She would always find ways to make best use of things that one would look and think are ready to be disposed of.

I always got interested in the various home improvements projects with which my parents were involved. Following their example, I also started to get creative and learn to do things by myself, such as building a badminton net and setting it up in our backyard, using materials I had on hand. I also learned how to service motors by regularly servicing my father's scooter for some pocket money. My biggest project and the one I was most proud of, however, was building a home gym from scratch. It cost almost nothing and used materials I found around the house.

As they say time flies and here my father was soon approaching his retirement. I observed how much more actively involved he was with his finances, constantly planning out how things should be handled after his retirement in order to still fund his children's educations. One Sunday my parents were driving back home on their scooter and were hit by another vehicle. It was a life-changing day in our family— my father suffered serious brain hemorrhage and passed away. God showed some mercy and our mother survived the accident. I was 17 and had lost my biggest inspiration in life.

I was also lucky because about three years before my father passed away, he had been giving me a lot of insight on how to manage finances and how he had prepared his to take care of our family and our educations. With his passing I became the "man of the house," even though I had a long way to go. It took us time to emerge from the shock, but we so with all the good memories and wisdom that our father embedded in us.

In 1994, I received my Bachelor of Science in physics . My dream was to major in computer engineering, but I was not selected after my school because of my low grades, so I settled on pursuing my undergraduate degree in physics. Once I was done, I applied for the entrance exam for a post-graduation computers diploma and managed to clear the exam as one of the 35 candidates across the entire state selected for this course. I received that post-graduate diploma in 1995. I was entering a new phase of life after completing my education. I was definitely nervous, but excited, to be starting my professional journey.

In July 1995, I started my first job, as a computer software programmer trainee with a salary of 2,000 rupees (Rs) per month. In today's market if converted to US dollars it would be approximately between $40 - $50. I tried to apply to the same company where I did my internship but was not selected as they needed only one person and there were four interns. So I went out and started hunting for a trainee or entry level software development position.

In my initial year of working, I decided I wanted to buy a motor bike and a computer for myself. I did not have enough money saved up yet, so I asked my mother help fund some of the expenses. My mother agreed to fund me, but only gave me Rs 50,000 (approximately $1,000

- $1,200) and told me to decide how to best make use of that money. She said I could buy the best computer with all features I want and use that for work and as I make more money, buy the motorbike for myself later or put that money towards buying the motorbike first. It did not take much consideration, as I felt more strongly about having a computer. I decided to buy the fully featured computer that included multi-media kit. I also managed to get a low-end scooter that served my commuting needs. This was one of my first situations that taught me to understand my wants as opposed to my needs.

By early 1997, I decided to become an independent consultant after switching a couple jobs between 1995 and 1997. By this time, I was making almost Rs 12,000 (approximately $250 - $300) per month.

In June 1997, after three attempts in three consecutive years, I finally cleared the entrance exam and was selected as a Master of Business Adminstration (MBA) candidate at B.K. School of Business Management. I picked the part-time program with evening classes that would allow me to continue working my day job. My primary drive to join MBA program was to help me with some leadership skills that would enable greater opportunities in entry-level management positions within technology.

By early 1998, I was convinced that there was more career potential in technology if I traveled abroad or found work with a multi-national firm. With that in mind, I decided to join an employer that had overseas presence in Singapore, Canada and the United States. My main motivation was to gain experience dealing with overseas client projects. My initial client was in Nigeria, followed by a client in Canada. Dealing clients overseas meant working around the clock and it became very challenging to juggle between that job and evening MBA studies. However, at this time, I was making almost Rs 25,000 (approximately $500 - $600) per month.

By late 1998, I was making efforts to travel overseas on a project assignment, and finally got a break, not only with my current employer, but also from another US-based technology consulting company where one of my former bosses from India was employed. My ultimate dream was to work in the US so I immediately accepted the offer of the US-based firm to join them in January 1999 and had to dropout from my MBA program. At last, with the support of my mother and sisters and this job offer, my dream journey had begun!

My finances prior to 1999:

In over three years of working in India, while I could not build enough on my assets, I did achieve financial freedom by paying off in full any of my personal loans as soon as I could! The chart below shows how I stood as of December 1998 with my finances. At that time in India, this was a decent middle class income.

Year	Prior to 1999
Net Earnings	$5,000 - $10,000
Total Retirement Savings	$500
Total Loans & Mortgages	$0 (All Loans Paid off)
Total Net Worth	$0 - $5,000
Total Assets	$0 - $5,000

1999

On January 29, I boarded the flight from India to the United States with $500 in cash and travelers check. I landed in Virginia at 2: 40 p.m. It was an indescribable feeling to have one of my lifelong dreams come true merely 15 days before my 25th birthday.

I took a cab from the airport directly to my employer's office, as I had been advised. Upon reaching the office, I spent my very first dollars—$8.50 to the cab driver, rounded to $10 to include tip.

Initial Months

My employer provided me with the option to stay in one of their guesthouses for four weeks while they found a client placement for me and I searched for a more permanent accommodation.

My search for an apartment started with few key things in mind. I wanted a reasonably priced accommodation that I could share with roommates. Distance was important for me—I wanted it to be fairly close to both my client and employer site. I also narrowed my search to apartments that did not have heavy penalties for breaking contract and did not have excessive utility costs. A basic gym would be a plus, but was not a necessity. Overall, I wanted to find something that would be in the $500-$600 (per month, per person) range.

Keeping the above in mind, the first thing I did was ask around in my new circle of friends and colleagues for roommates and for apartment hunting advice. In no time, I had three coworkers agree to finding a shared accommodation for all of us. After two weekends of visiting various apartment complexes, three of us settled on a 12-month contract with deal that gave us one month for free. It worked out to $380 per person per month, plus utilities. Our complex had a very basic gym, too! Unfortunately, because none of us had established credit in the US, we had to pay two months (instead of one) for our security deposit.

Then it was time to establish a credit line. I was able to apply for a credit card through my employer and their affiliate credit union. I got my first credit card approved with a credit limit of $2,000. Though I was tempted to go on a spending spree, I knew my first purchase had to be a car. It was a necessity for me because my client site was about five miles away from the nearest public transportation station. I had been carpooling with a colleague for the first few weeks, but I needed my own vehicle for all my other non-work related tasks.

When my search started I had to differentiate between luxuries and necessities. I started my search with few things in mind. I wanted a new, automatic transmission car that had decent gas mileage and good resale value. I was convinced that a used car might require more maintenance and at this time there were no good extended warranty options available (which was an important deciding factor for me). I also wanted something that would have a down payment of less than

$3,000 and a monthly loan payment of no more than $400.

With that in mind, I started visiting dealerships around town. One of my friends joined me on these trips as he was also interested in buying a new car. Our two-person approach actually worked to our benefit because dealers ended up making better offers when they knew they would be selling two cars. We also had some luck with our timing, as the new models were coming in and they had more aggressive deals with the previous year's models. After lots of research and some test-driving, I finally settled for a Honda Civic. I managed to lock on a five-year loan with monthly installments of $267. Because I had just turned 25, I was also able to escape the high insurance rates for drivers under 25! (I should also mention that although it took me two tries, I got my driver's license in the first couple of weeks of my arrival because it doubled as an important identification document.)

Next, it was time to settle into the apartment. Moving was not much of a hassle as all of us had very little belongings. With no packing and no planning, it was a quick and easy move from the guesthouse to the new apartment. Our biggest issue was deciding who would get the bigger room and who would settle for the smaller ones. In trying to keep things fair, we played a game in which the winner picked the room they wanted first. I happened to win the game and picked the biggest room.

We then laid down some ground rules for our apartment. We decided that each person was responsible for cleaning one shared area of the apartment each week. This meant that the kitchen, living room, and dining room rotated amongst the three of us. We also decided to take turns taking out the trash, running the dishwasher, and cooking meals. That last one worked for us because we all wanted to eat at home and could agree on sharing groceries. Utilities were split evenly among the three of us. We had to pay for electricity, water, and gas and managed to keep the total amount per person per month under $50. We all agreed that we needed a telephone line and internet, and split the installation and monthly fees for those as well.

The key to my survival in my new country was ensuring that I have a happy employer who values my work as an employee. This proved to be a challenge at times because I came here with very minimal background knowledge of the working culture in the US. I also had a bit of a Hinglish accent. Hinglish is a slang term for the Hindi-accent flecked English that new immigrants have. This was enough to make me anxious about entering the workplace. I knew I needed to follow the work ethics that I developed back in India that helped grow in my professional career there. Although I had a language barrier on my side, I went about the office as I had in India, by making sure I greeted colleagues with a smile, by staying honest, dedicated and focused, and by continually working hard to compensate for my shortcomings. I listened well before I spoke up and I analyzed thoroughly before I made any conclusions. Additionally, it is always important to recognize and acknowledge the hard work of others. One thank you note can say a lot! I had also learned to be flexible and to entertain unanticipated requests from those higher up. If I did something wrong, I came upfront to admit to my mistake with an apology. I also learned that positive sentences are a very powerful way of communication (i.e. "I will do my best;" "I will try;" "Yes sure, it's doable, but might need more time and research;" "I will be happy to help," etc) and that negative sentences are not so useful ("I don't know;" "No, not possible;" "Don't ask me," etc). Above all, I found that communicating often and precisely was helpful, as well as being open to feedback and sharing future career goals with my boss. With all of this in mind, and a healthy dose of confidence, I was able to adjust quickly to my new environment.

As the year was ending, I had a small brush with fate. I was driving back from my client site one day and felt my car lose friction with the road. I had slipped on some black ice. In my panic, I slammed on the brakes and lost control of the car, spinning in three circles on the road before coming to a stop. I was fortunate enough to have been in the center lane and also the only car on the road, thus I did not hit the shoulders or any other cars. It took a few moments for me to regain my compusure and make sense of what I needed to do. My car had turned off, so I tried to start it again, but it would not start. Again, I panicked. I put on my emergency blinkers and a truck driver came to my aid. He then approached me to check if I was ok and my response was, I was ok but I guess my car was still in shock :-) ! He then advised me to turn off all of the electronics and lights in the car. I took his advice, and sure enough, the car started. He made sure I was fine before driving away. I thanked him and to this day, am thankful that he stopped to help me out. It was a startling experience, and an interesting way to wrap up my first year in the US.

Fun, Hobbies, Entertainment, and Travel Activities:

Because I had just moved to a new country and a new area, a lot of my leisure time and weekend activities revolved around exploring my environment. I found a few friends who had the same interests, and together we took weekend road trips to New York City, Atlantic City and sought out much of Washington, D.C.'s offerings. Road trips proved to be a cost effective and entertaining. We got to see much of the eastern seaboard and Virginia this way. In addition to visiting cities, we would plan camping and hiking trips through the Shenandoah Valley.

Financial Insights:

Before I highlight on some financial details for this year, I wanted to introduce my Smart Savings theory. Smart Savings is not the actual dollar savings generated, but the prevention of likely expenses that one might otherwise incur. However, by doing research and spending wisely (in some instances this might mean spending more), it generates larger savings in the long term. As you will uncover in my book, the smart savings approach helped me significantly every year. Below I have defined some terms you will see throughout my book.

- Net Earnings: Includes salary, bonus, interests, special compensations, night and weekend job earnings, business earnings, insurance claims and more

- Spendings: Includes expenses and investments

- Net Savings: Actual Savings generated after excluding expenses and investment spendings

- Retirement Savings: not included as part of the net earnings

- Yearly Smart Savings: Smarts Savings assumed for the given year

- Total Smart Savings: Year-by-year incremental assumed total of smart savings

- Notes: details about how I achieved smart savings

Below you will see that while my net earnings were just between $25K and $50K, I still managed to achieve a yearly net savings between $10K and $25K. In other words, I achieved almost 50% in yearly net savings against my yearly net earnings.

This year I generated over $10,000 in smart savings, with about 50% generated from purchasing an economical car model, sharing an accommodation, utilities, and groceries. Avoiding eating out too much also helped me generate a significant amount of smart savings.

At this point, my assets and net worth were under $25,000 and my biggest financial burden was my car loan (which was slightly above $10,000).

Expense Categories	Spending	SmartS $	SmartS %	Notes
Home Buy & Loan	0.0%	-	0.0%	
Car Buy & Loan	35.4%	2,400	21.2%	+$: Employer Loan, Car Model
Rent	26.2%	3,600	31.8%	+$: Roommates/Shared
Utilities (E,W & G)	4.5%	960	8.5%	+$: Shared, Usage conscious
Grocery	4.1%	600	5.3%	+$: Shared
Gas	5.4%	240	2.1%	+$: Carpool
Insurance	7.9%	-	0.0%	
Internet	0.0%	240	2.1%	+$: In 1999 Dial-up felt sufficient
Cell Phone	0.0%	600	5.3%	+$: Was not necessary yet
Cable/Dish	0.0%	480	4.2%	+$: Local channels sufficed
Lunch/Dinner Outs	1.2%	1,440	12.7%	+$: Cooking home
Hobby	0.0%	-	0.0%	
Travel & Entertainment	4.8%	175	1.5%	+$: Group Deals, Group Travel
International Calls	3.3%	-	0.0%	
Home Improvements	4.1%	300	2.6%	+$: Yard/Garage Sale, DIY
Donations	0.0%	-	0.0%	
Stocks	0.0%	-	0.0%	
Maintenance & Services	0.0%	300	2.6%	+$: Got three years of free car service
Personal Business	0.0%	-	0.0%	
Miscellaneous	3.1%	-	0.0%	
Total	**100.0%**	**11,335**	**100.0%**	

AVG % SMARTS*: 0 21 31 8 5 2 0 2 5 4 12 0 1 0 2 0 0 2 0 0

AVG % SPENDS: 0 35 26 4 4 5 7 0 0 0 1 0 4 3 4 0 0 0 0 3

100% 80% 60% 40% 20% 0%

AVG % SMARTS* / AVG % SPENDS*

Home Buy & Loan, Car & Loan, Rent, Utilities (E, W & G), Grocery, Gas, Insurance, Internet, Cell Phone, Cable/Dish, Lunch/Dinner Outs, Hobby, Travel & Entertainment, International Calls, Home Improvements, Donations, Stocks, Maintenance & Services, Personal Business, Miscellaneous

*SMARTS=Smart Savings

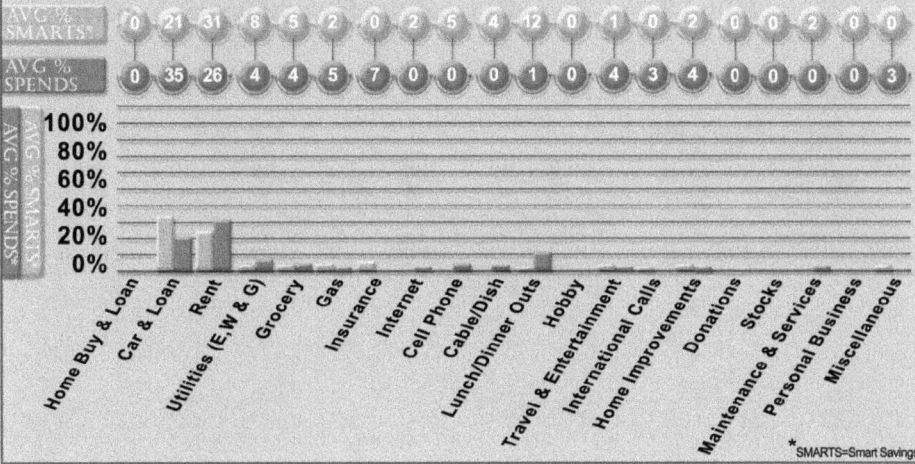

FINANCIAL INSIGHTS:

NET EARNINGS	NET SPENDS/ EXPENSES	NET SAVINGS	RETIREMENT SAVINGS	NET SMARTS*	TOTAL SMARTS*	TOTAL LOANS & MORTG	TOTAL NETWORTH	TOTAL ASSETS
$25K - $50K	$10K - $25K	$10K - $25K	$0 - $5K	$10K - $25K	$10K - $25K	$5 - $10K	$10K - $25K	$10K - $25K

Year	1999
Net Earnings	$25,000 - $50,000
Yearly Net Spending & Investment	$10,000 - $25,000
Yearly Net Savings	$10,000 - $25,000
Yearly Retirement Savings	$0 - $5,000
Yearly Smart Savings	$10,000 - $25,000
Total Smart Savings	$10,000 - $25,000
Total Loans & Mortgages	$5,000 - $10,000
Total Net Worth	$10,000 - $25,000
Total Assets	$10,000 - $25,000

Personal Insights

This is how I gauged some aspects of my lifestyle. You will find this at end of each year as I progress through my journey.

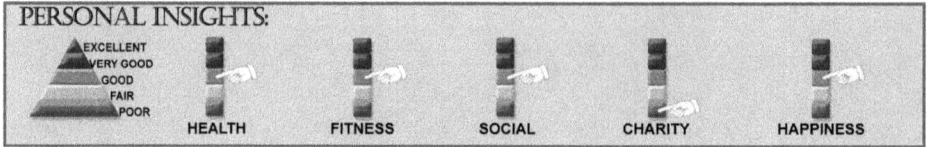

PERSONAL INSIGHTS:

EXCELLENT
VERY GOOD
GOOD
FAIR
POOR

HEALTH   FITNESS   SOCIAL   CHARITY   HAPPINESS

2000

A simple fact that is hard to learn is that the time to save money is when you have some.

- Joe Moore

This year started with a bang—2000 was the year of the Y2K craze, so most techies and computer people remember that new year's eve as the one we spent on call to ensure nothing went awry. It was a fun night, and I am sure most people in the technology world have a story to tell about that night.

Coming back to the bang, the story I want to share, I was driving in my new car (now almost 8-9 months old in the early 2000) coming back from my client site one evening, and I heard a bang that shook me. A big sports truck decided to change lanes without looking around properly and hit my car, not realizing that I was slowing down because of the red light ahead of us. We pulled aside and I ran to check on the other side to see how bad the damage was. Unfortunately, both of my right side doors were smashed badly. My nicely maintained new car was damaged and I was angry—until I saw an elderly couple step out of the truck. Immediately, my anger subsided and I realized that this was an honest mistake. I was not sure what to do now, but then remembered I should just call 911. Guess what? I had no cell phone. This was my first time I realized that a cell phone is not a luxury, but something of a necessity. Within that week, I bought my very first cell phone.

In early January, my recruiter asked me to start applying for my Green Card since the company would be sponsoring it. I initially resisted, saying that my goal was to return to India after three years of working, so I had no reason for me to even bother with it. My recruiter countered that he had heard this from several other employees in the past and most of them later regretted their decision to not apply or get a head start on the process. He continued explaining that there is nothing to lose by applying as I would have the option to keep the Green Card or not, if and when I decide to go back. I appreciated his advice and immediately started my Green Card application. Fourteen years into my stay in the States and I am still grateful for his advice and the decision to apply for it.

At this point I had another item that became a necessity: a more robust Internet connection. My expanded role at the client site was the reason for this becoming a necessity. I became part of the primary development team that was responsible for an around-the-clock production up-time which meant being able to support any issues that surfaced, even in the middle of the night. I convinced my other roommates about getting a cable modem Internet connection and we got it going in no time.

In February, it was time for my first yearly review at work. I had been tracking each and every note of appreciation from my clients during the course of the entire last year. In a way, I was already gearing myself up for the review. This translates into me trying to do my level best to meet expectations of the clients at every level resulting into a good recognition received during the course of last year. Before I went for my review meeting, I forwarded a summary of my achievements to my vertical head and the human resources department head, giving them enough time to review them on top of the usual appraisal document.

On the day of review, conversations went well regarding what I would like to do in the coming year for my personal and technical development. I also requested my boss' candid feedback on my overall performance for the past year and areas he thought I could do better. This is an important piece of the review process as it helps you to understand perspective of your seniors, peers, and client. Afterwards, I also met with the HR head. He, too, was pleased with my performance and my efforts, and we were able to negotiate a pay raise. I believe that my honesty with them and my openness to hearing their feedback and criticism laid good groundwork for this conversation. It is important to keep in mind that negotiation is an art and a two-way process.

Around the same time I got my raise, I was also becoming better friends with another consultant who was heavily involved with the stock market. He really caught my attention and I started chatting with him more and more about stocks. He gave me some insight into how he would invest in different companies. He went on to tell me about how his stock profile multiplied tenfold in a matter of a couple of years. When I heard that, I went ahead and opened my first ever stocks account to experiment with the hopes that I would soon see tenfold returns, too.

I decided to set aside a little less than $3,000 to invest in this market and try out my luck. I say "my luck" because my knowledge was extremely limited. I took some advice from my friends to see what stocks they were investing in and accordingly made my own investing decisions. I invested in three or four different companies by splitting my money equally in each, but put none into mutual funds. Apparently I was not watching the market well (something that stemmed from my lack of understanding) and suffered a major loss of almost all my invested money. This was a big blow to me and almost to this day I stayed away from the stock market!

I learned a few lessons from this financial mishap though. I learned to not imitate others and to do my own research before investing. Investing in high-risk stocks and going for short-term gains are only a good idea when you really understand the market. Also, going for the most popular mutual funds is the better option when you are just entering the market. Lastly, always be sure to spread your investments across different industries instead of focusing on just one industry. High risk may bring high returns, low risk may bring low returns.

At this point, I was a quite upset and turned to my friends for advice. One of them mentioned that the only thing he invests in is his 401(k). After listening to his reasoning, I realized that I should have started this almost a year ago through my company. Though I felt behind, it is always to start later than to never start when it comes to saving money and planning your financials wisely. After one and a half years with my company, I set up my 401(k) account. The focus of a 401(k) is to set up long-term returns in preparation for retirement. Your company invests a certain percent to the amount you invest (each company has their own set contribution percentage), so it is a low-risk investment. Additionally, the investment is tax-free.

While we are on the topic of retirement, here are some more tips that I wish to share with you.

Retirement Savings Tips

There is a very high chance that you will want to retire at some point, so it is best—as with any type of saving—to start as early as you possibly can. Set aside a certain amount for your retirement fund. Personally, I would recommend to invest in 401(k) at least equivalent to what your employer offers in match. Set a savings goal so that by the time you want to retire, it will pay you back like a decent monthly salary for the rest of your life. This is tricky, but the key is to start early. With bonds and compound interest, these small savings can multiply to what you need in few decades. Just commit yourself! As with stocks, it is a good idea to diversify your savings approach (as I will discuss later on in the book). Keep in mind that a 401(k) is not the only savings option. Explore the Roth IRA and company-specific options as well. Aside from saving, manage your mortgage well and plan it to pay off before 30 years. Ideally, you would close it five to 10 years before retirement. Lastly, research life insurance plans that pay you back after you reach retirement age.

MENTION: Make sure that you explore options of tuition funds and save for your children as applicable. Best way to know what options are available at any point of time is by chatting with your social circle and surely with your employer too.

Around October, I was thinking about how the interest I was paying on my car loan and if I could avoid it by paying off the rest of it in cash. I took a look at my savings and at the balance on my loan, and saw that I had enough to write a check for the remaining amount. I realized that if I did this, my emergency cash savings would be depleted, but I decided to move forward with that decision. It was the biggest check I had written at this point in my life—nearly $10,000! However, after I paid it I had one less burden off my back that I had been carrying. That, and the knowledge that I was not accumulating interest, made the decision worth it. Though it was a risk, it was a calculated risk. I did not jeopardize any aspect of my life or finances by making this decision; rather, I only stepped outside of limits I had set. Sometimes these risks are worth it. The key is to make an informed decision that will have greater rewards than going the traditional route.

There are three important things I have learned through the years of paying loans that are worth thinking about. First, pay high of a down payment as you possibly can. Second, be very punctual with your payments and be sure to never miss an installment. Third, whenever you have the chance, add a slightly higher principal to your loan payments as it helps in reducing the overall interest you will pay. This is how your savings add up—penny by penny, dime by dime, dollar by dollar!

After making all these payments that slowly and firmly estab-
lished my life in the US, I spent a little more and took a trip back to
India in November. It was my first time returning in nearly two years.
I was proud of my accomplishments up to this point, and was eager to
go home and see my mother and sisters for a little bit.

Financial Insights:

Almost 40% of my net spending and investment was related to
paying off the car loan that resulted into a lesser net savings. With loan
payoff, it was first step towards building my asset.

This year also I managed to achieve over $10,000 in smart savings.
While paying off my auto loan contributed to the largest chunk of my
smart savings (almost 40%) the remaining smart savings were generated from my shared accommodation, including utilities and groceries.

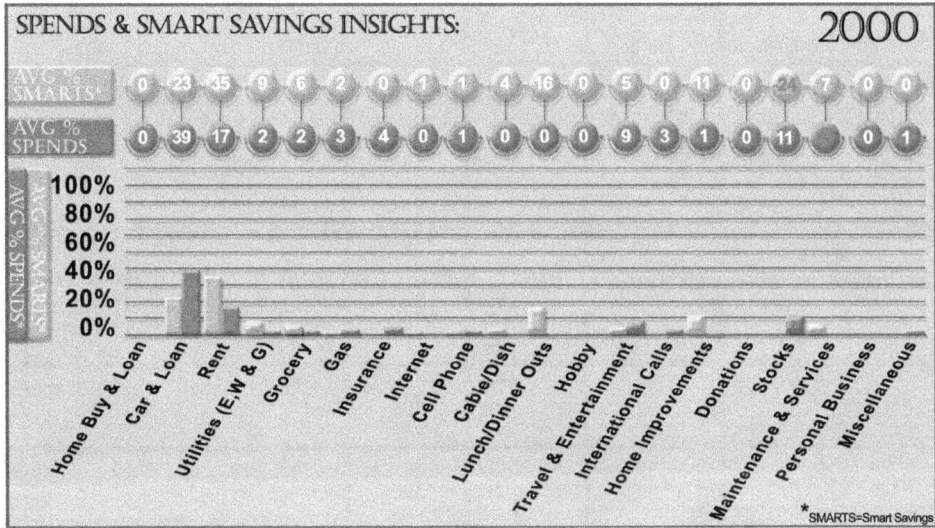

SPENDS & SMART SAVINGS INSIGHTS: 2000

| AVG % SMARTS: | 0 | 23 | 35 | 9 | 6 | 2 | 0 | 1 | 1 | 4 | 16 | 0 | 5 | 0 | 11 | 0 | 24 | 7 | 0 | 0 |
| AVG % SPENDS | 0 | 39 | 17 | 2 | 2 | 3 | 4 | 0 | 1 | 0 | 0 | 0 | 9 | 3 | 1 | 0 | 11 | | 0 | 1 |

* SMARTS=Smart Savings

Expense Categories	Spending	SmartS $	SmartS %	Notes
Home Buy & Loan	0.0%	-	0.0%	
Car Buy & Loan	39.4%	2,400	23.9%	+$: Paid-off car loan, saved on Interest
Rent	17.3%	3,600	35.9%	+$: When roommates moved, new joined
Utilities (E,W & G)	2.7%	960	9.6%	+$: Shared, Usage conscious
Grocery	2.5%	600	6.0%	+$: Shared
Gas	3.4%	240	2.4%	+$: Carpool
Insurance	4.4%	-	0.0%	
Internet	0.7%	150	1.5%	+$: Shared
Cell Phone	1.5%	150	1.5%	+$: Group Deal, Contract
Cable/Dish	0.0%	480	4.8%	+$: Local Channels sufficient
Lunch/Dinner Outs	0.6%	1,650	16.5%	+$: Cooking home
Hobby	0.0%	-	0.0%	
Travel & Enter-tainment	9.5%	500	5.0%	+$: Group Deals, Group Travel
International Calls	3.7%	-	0.0%	
Home Improve-ments	1.1%	1,100	11.0%	+$: Limited necessity furniture ONLY
Donations	0.0%	-	0.0%	
Stocks	11.4%	(2,500)	-24.9%	-$: Bad stock selections, Bubble Burst
Maintenance & Services	0.0%	700	7.0%	+$: Discount Bargain & free services
Personal Busi-ness	0.0%	-	0.0%	
Miscellaneous	1.7%	-	0.0%	
Total	100.0%	11,335	100.0%	

FINANCIAL INSIGHTS:

$25K - $50K	$25K - $50K	$0 - $5K	$0 - $5K	$10K - $25K	$10K - $25K	$0 - $5K	$25K - $50K	$25K - $50K
NET EARNINGS	NET SPENDS/ EXPENSES	NET SAVINGS	RETIREMENT SAVINGS	NET SMARTS*	TOTAL SMARTS*	TOTAL LOANS & MORTG	TOTAL NETWORTH	TOTAL ASSETS

Year	2000
Net Earnings	$25,000 - $50,000
Yearly Net Spending & Investment	$25,000 - $50,000
Yearly Net Savings	$0 - $5,000
Yearly Retirement Savings	$0 - $5,000
Yearly Smart Savings	$10,000 - $25,000
Total Smart Savings	$10,000 - $25,000
Total Loans & Mortgages	$0 - $5,000
Total Net Worth	$25,000 - $50,000
Total Assets	$25,000 - $50,000

PERSONAL INSIGHTS:

EXCELLENT
VERY GOOD
GOOD
FAIR
POOR

HEALTH	FITNESS	SOCIAL	CHARITY	HAPPINESS

29

2001

It's not your salary that makes you rich, it's your spending habits.
- Charles A. Jaffe

My new year started on a plane flying across the oceans, celebrating 2001 at 40,000 feet in the sky! In December 2000, my company picked me as a representative to go over to Europe and help out with another client. It was a surprise when my vertical head reached out and said that I would be leaving my client at the time as there was a more urgent need at their European site. Within a few days, my Schengen Visa was prepared and in less than a month I was on my way to Dusseldorf, Germany. Despite the communication challenges I faced (I had never taken a German language class in my life!), I was excited for this unexpected turn in my life and professional career.

I got quickly acquainted with my client and the client site, but the highlight of my time in Germany was that I was able to travel to a different German city or other nearby country each weekend. The biggest difference was the work schedule—at this client site in Germany, instead of a nine-to-five workday, they worked from 8 am to almost 8 pm Monday through Wednesday and were off of work by noon on Thursday. I adopted this schedule as well, which worked to my benefit by giving me more time when I was traveling. In addition to travelling around Europe every few weeks, I made a trip back to States so that I could take care of my rent, bills and other things that needed my attention. During all these travels, I made sure to collect my airline miles and hotel points whenever I could. In doing so, I was able to collect enough points to buy me a ticket to India as well—a $1,500 value at the time.

After all of this traveling, I became pretty efficient in packing. Here are some tips I learned that will help you get the most out of your time and money when visiting a new city or country.

Traveling Tips

Make a list of items you will need regardless of traveling. Keep this list as a reference guide so you will not have to deal with having to run out to buy a razor or toothbrush, or have to deal with incurring silly costs by forgetting to pack socks or underwear. Also before you go somewhere, do some upfront research about places you would like to see or hidden gems around the city. Look into how far they are from each other and how you will get there. Transportation costs are not limited to your arrival and departure and can add up quickly—do some research to find out the most efficient mode of transportation. For example, in the States, I did all my traveling by car, since I owned one and the biggest cost was gas and the biggest benefit was being able to go wherever I wanted in the city without relying on public transportation. In Europe, however, I traveled everywhere by their extensive rail system. Look into these and see what your options are.

As far as accommodations, try not to get lured into staying at the nicest hotel or the historical hotel if you are on a budget. Though it seems like it would be a good experience, all you will be using it for is sleeping and showering. When traveling with friends, you can share hotel rooms. When traveling solo, look into less expensive options or deals.

When you are in the city, it is worth stopping by a tourist information center to get some information. Oftentimes they can point you to good tours and landmarks and tell you if an attraction will be especially busy at a certain time or on a certain day. This information is invaluable when you want to make the most of your time! If you are not keen on visiting tourist attractions, see if you can find a walking route or a bike tour. Some cities are the attraction, and simply being there is an experience.

Credit Card Rewards Tips

As I mentioned above, I was able to purchase my ticket to India using credit card rewards. I have enjoyed having a credit card with a reward system and have cashed out the rewards throughout the years (up to $3,000 at one point down the line). However, there are some things that you should be aware when dealing with credit card rewards. First and foremost, even though these competitive reward systems are nice, do not get so carried away in trying to earn them that you end up spending more or making impulsive purchases. That will be more costly than the money you save using your rewards! On the same note, try not to impulsively cash out your rewards as soon as they add up or there is an offer to redeem them for something. Ask if you really want that item or if you just want to get it because it's available. Also try not to have too many cards with thin rewards—if possible, consolidate your credit cards under one point system (this will require some research). Lastly, keep an eye on the expiration date for redeeming your points—it can be easy to lose all the points if you do not redeem them within a certain time period.

I have compiled these tips into a handy reference guide at the back of the book (Travel Tips) so you may turn to them whenever you need.

After my stint in Europe, coming back to the US felt like a homecoming of sorts. Though my true roots were in India, I had come to see America as my home away from home. Unfortunately, I was not received very warmly, as I came back to my first bench period (a term for the period when a consultant is not on any project and only helping with internal matters). Two weeks into my bench period and in the midst of the dotcom bubble bursting, I was called once again to the HR department. This time, I knew the conversation would not be pleasant. I was requested to take voluntary salary cut of almost 12% in order to help the company sail through these tougher times and to take up with a client in Boston. I had peers who had lost their jobs and, due to being in the country on an H-1B visa, had to return home. Taking a pay cut and going to Boston for a while did not seem very bad in comparison.

Before even I could feel the warmth of being back in the US, I was on my way to a new city for my next assignment. I landed in Boston and opted to stay in the company's guesthouse in order to save money on hotel expenses that would be charged to the company. This gesture was appreciated by the company and resulted in a bonus for me down the line. This assignment was a few weeks long, so I knew I had to keep an eye out for longer projects while I was on this one. These weeks passed, the project concluded, and it was time for me to get on board onto something new. I was able to secure another, longer project in Boston again, with the same lower hourly rate. However, I readily accepted this project, because I knew now that I did not really want to return to India anymore. Also, given that I was on an H-1B visa, I could not easily switch companies without losing my visa and Green Card employer sponsorship.

Around late July or early August, I started on this longer project. Though I was going to be in Boston for an extended period this time around, I still opted to stay in the company guesthouse as I had not moved out of my apartment in Virginia yet. I had strong ties to Herndon, Virginia, where I first moved and would always find myself going back there (a 16-hour trek by car) for one reason or another.

This year we were also affected by the events of September 11. We had been working for probably half an hour or so before we started hearing about the Twin Towers getting hit in New York. I was very touched by this event and was very closely monitoring the overall incident that knowingly or unknowingly I built up flying phobia—a fear that stayed with me for years until I sought treatment.

Financial Insights:

I strongly believe that my smart savings effort for consecutive 3 years, really helped me to take a leap in my asset buildup from $25,000-$50,000 to $50,000-$100,000. This was huge for me because, it in a way was starting to build a small but valuable safety financial net for me.

This year I generated net savings somewhere in the range of $25,000-$50,000, which was nearly 60% of my total income. I was able to save this much mainly because I had no outstanding loans or a mortgage to pay off. For the third consecutive year, I generated a smart savings average of about $10,000, mostly because I was still living in a shared accommodation.

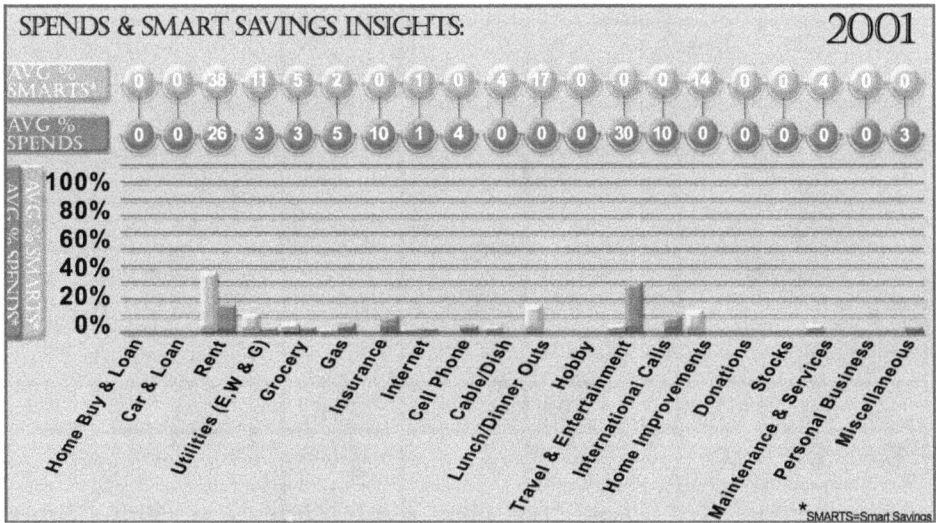

SPENDS & SMART SAVINGS INSIGHTS: 2001

	Home Buy & Loan	Car & Loan	Rent	Utilities (E,W & G)	Grocery	Gas	Insurance	Internet	Cell Phone	Cable/Dish	Lunch/Dinner Outs	Hobby	Travel & Entertainment	International Calls	Home Improvements	Donations	Stocks	Maintenance & Services	Personal Business	Miscellaneous
AVG % SMARTS*	0	0	38	11	5	2	0	1	0	4	17	0	0	0	14	0	0	4	0	0
AVG % SPENDS	0	0	26	3	3	5	10	1	4	0	0	0	30	10	0	0	0	0	0	3

*SMARTS=Smart Savings

Expense Categories	Spending	SmartS $	SmartS %	Notes
Home Buy & Loan	0.0%	-	0.0%	
Car Buy & Loan	0.0%	-	0.0%	
Rent	26.3%	4,000	38.2%	+$: Company accommodation; public storage
Utilities (E,W & G)	3.5%	1,200	11.5%	+$: Mostly on company travel
Grocery	3.1%	600	5.7%	+$: Eating outside on company travel
Gas	5.3%	240	2.3%	+$: Rental car on company travel
Insurance	10.1%	-	0.0%	
Internet	1.6%	150	1.4%	+$: Shared
Cell Phone	4.2%	-	0.0%	
Cable/Dish	0.0%	480	4.6%	+$: Local channels sufficient
Lunch/Dinner Outs	0.7%	1,800	17.2%	+$: Cooking home
Hobby	0.0%	-	0.0%	
Travel & Entertainment	30.7%	-	0.0%	
International Calls	10.5%	-	0.0%	
Home Improvements	0.0%	1,500	14.3%	+$: Limited to necessary furniture only
Donations	0.0%	-	0.0%	
Stocks	0.0%	-	0.0%	
Maintenance & Services	0.0%	500	4.8%	+$: Timely car servicing, discounts
Personal Business	0.0%	-	0.0%	
Miscellaneous	3.9%	-	0.0%	
Total	100.0%	10,470	100.0%	

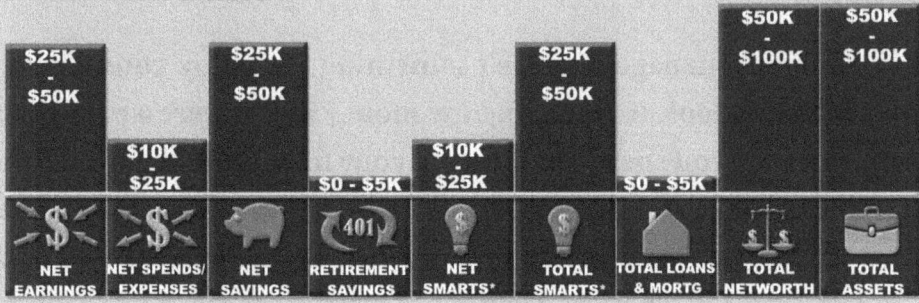

FINANCIAL INSIGHTS:

Year	2001
Net Earnings	$25,000 - $50,000
Yearly Net Spending & Investment	$10,000 - $25,000
Yearly Net Savings	$25,000 - $50,000
Yearly Retirement Savings	$0 - $5,000
Yearly Smart Savings	$10,000 - $25,000
Total Smart Savings	$25,000 - $50,000
Total Loans & Mortgages	$0 - $5,000
Total Net Worth	$50,000 - $100,000
Total Assets	$50,000 - $100,000

PERSONAL INSIGHTS:

37

2002

If money management isn't something you enjoy, consider my perspective. I look at managing my money as if it were a part-time job. The time you spend monitoring your finances will pay off. You can make real money by cutting expenses and earning more interest on savings and investments. I'd challenge you to find a part-time job where you could potentially earn as much money for just an hour or two of your time.

- Laura D. Adams

I was driving back to Boston from New Year's celebrations in Virginia when I saw lights in my rearview mirror. This year started out by giving me my very first speeding ticket! The unexpected expense aside, I also received a point on my license—these are the small things that lead to higher insurance premiums and make it worth having a clean driving record!

So I was back in Boston and back in the company's guesthouse. A few weeks in, they asked me to start looking for my own rented apartment as they were not renewing the lease on the guesthouse and still wanted me to stay in Boston for the remainder of project. I started my hunt by asking around for people who were looking for roommates— just a place I could easily and quickly sublet for a few months. I gave notice to my roommates in Herndon as well, and asked a friend to change my address to his address (also in Virginia) for the time being since I knew I wanted to head back there eventually. In Boston, I ended up finding a small unit to rent with two other roommates in the same complex as my company's former guesthouse.

I went back to Herndon briefly to pick up my things from my apartment and hold a quick garage sale. It was a way to lighten my load before I put things in storage and gave me a chance to make some money while saying goodbye to all of my friends. Garage sales can actually be profitable if they are organized and advertised properly. Make sure to keep an eye on the forecast for the week before your garage sale. Though you cannot predict the weather for the day of the sale, you can usually avoid larger storms or excessively cold fronts this way. If you want to give some things away or know that friends would be interested in certain goods, have them come by the day before to go through your items. Also, be sure you have plenty of small bills and coins on hand. I went to the bank and got about $50 in one- and five-dollar bills and rolled quarters. If you have the time, see if anyone on your street or block is interested in having a garage sale as well. This takes some more planning and coordinating schedules, but a multi-family or block yard sale will bring more traffic to the area and to your house as well. Lastly, advertise around your neighborhood and in the local grocery store with signs or fliers the week before your garage sale.

On the way back to Boston, I received yet another speeding ticket—after this one, I knew I was not being a careful driver and that I really needed to watch out unless I wanted my premiums to skyrocket.

Back in Boston, I also started shopping around for a gym membership. I was able to find a great deal at a top-of-the-line gym for only $29 per month if I bought a yearlong membership. When it comes to things like a gym membership, shop around and take advantage of seasonal deals. Do not be afraid to commit to a long-term membership because it will end up being less than a monthly membership—and will keep you motivated to go to the gym as well!

Late in the year my Boston client contract came to an end and I moved back to my base in Virginia. During the time I was in Boston, my company had a change in direction with the placement strategy and the technology tools I was working on were no more considered to be a good differentiator within the company for project placements. I stayed connected with my vertical head to remain informed on what are the new technology tools that would make next project placement easier. Based on the feedback, I started learning these new technology tools. Taking this approach of being flexible with learning new technology tools helped me to get placed quickly at another client site. If I was not on an employer-sponsored visa, I could have very well left the company to take on position matching my skills in hand at that time. But given that I was, exploring new career opportunities outside of the company was not an option. I think that staying flexible and learning new emerging market skills in one's area of expertise is always a plus for career growth. It worked well for me.

For a certain period of time after coming back from Boston I stayed in the company guesthouse of Herndon but soon enough I moved into a new place. At this time one of my HR resources and another consultant from my company, moved in with me as my roommates. With my new skills that I learned, I got placed on a local project at one of our client sites. I remember my initial days—I used to work late at the client site and then as soon as I was back, I would be again on my laptop working very hard to keep learning these new skills so that I could prove myself to be a valuable resource at the client site. Living with an HR manager ended up being useful here, as he witnessed my work habits and later placed a good word for me with upper management and senior staff.

This is the time when I thought of a savings concept that I named it as "Smart Savings Jar."

This concept worked very well for me. Essentially, it is a grown-up piggy bank. I had a large clear jar that became a visual reminder of my savings goal and a progress bar that showed my patience, my efforts, and eventual success. It is a very simple concept—I added certain denominations to the jar when I saved up a certain amount. It became a sort of game for me and a passive form of amusement that helped me save money, too!

- Whenever I saved $10 or less, I placed a penny in the jar

- Whenever I saved $11-$50, I placed a nickel in the jar

- Whenever I saved $51-$500, I placed a dime in the jar

- Whenever I saved more than $500, I placed a quarter in the jar.

This is neither meant to be a source of stress nor a game with hard and fast rules. It was just a way for me to quantify my savings on a smaller scale and have a place to keep my change. It took me almost couple of years before I filled my first jar, but that jar was really a visualization of hundreds of thousands of dollars!

Financial Insights:

Looking at the charts now, I feel, I could have done a little better job with building my retirement savings.

For the second year in a row, I managed to save nearly 60% of my net earnings, which generated about $25,000 - $50,000. This year I reached a little under $10,000 in smart savings primarily because we had fewer roommates, which resulted in a small spike in shared costs such as rent, utilities, groceries, and the like. However, my remaining roommates and I moved into a smaller rental accommodation to save some money on our rent.

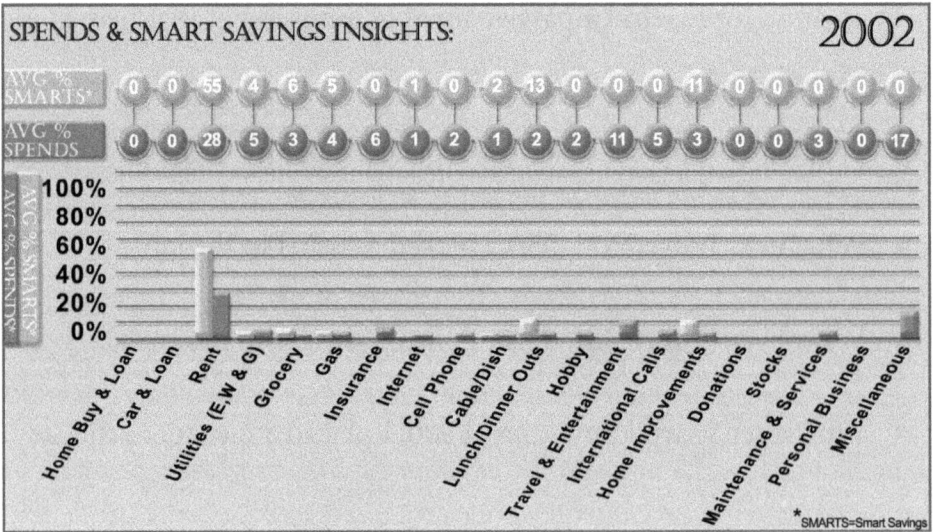

SPENDS & SMART SAVINGS INSIGHTS: 2002

	Home Buy & Loan	Car & Loan	Rent	Utilities (E,W & G)	Grocery	Gas	Insurance	Internet	Cell Phone	Cable/Dish	Lunch/Dinner Outs	Hobby	Travel & Entertainment	International Calls	Home Improvements	Donations	Stocks	Maintenance & Services	Personal Business	Miscellaneous
AVG % SMARTS	0	0	55	4	6	5	0	1	0	2	13	0	0	0	11	0	0	0	0	0
AVG % SPENDS	0	0	28	5	3	4	6	1	2	1	2	2	11	5	3	0	0	3	0	17

*SMARTS=Smart Savings

Expense Categories	Spending	SmartS $	SmartS %	Notes
Home Buy & Loan	0.0%	-	0.0%	
Car Buy & Loan	0.0%	-	0.0%	
Rent	28.5%	4,800	55.0%	+$: Shared Accomodation
Utilities (E,W & G)	5.0%	360	4.1%	+$: Shared, Usage conscious
Grocery	3.6%	600	6.9%	+$: Shared
Gas	4.3%	480	5.5%	+$: Accomodation near client site
Insurance	6.8%	-	0.0%	
Internet	1.1%	150	1.7%	+$: Shared
Cell Phone	2.9%	-	0.0%	+$: Group Deal, Contract
Cable/Dish	1.8%	180	2.1%	+$: Shared
Lunch/Dinner Outs	2.0%	1,152	13.2%	+$: Cooking home
Hobby	2.1%	-	0.0%	
Travel & Entertainment	11.9%	-	0.0%	+$: Group Deals, Group Travel
International Calls	5.7%	-	0.0%	
Home Improvements	3.0%	1,000	11.5%	+$: Limited necessity furniture ONLY
Donations	0.0%	-	0.0%	
Stocks	0.0%	-	0.0%	
Maintenance & Services	3.6%	-	0.0%	
Personal Business	0.0%	-	0.0%	
Miscellaneous	17.8%	-	0.0%	Includes expenses for Dependants
Total	100.0%	8,722	100.0%	

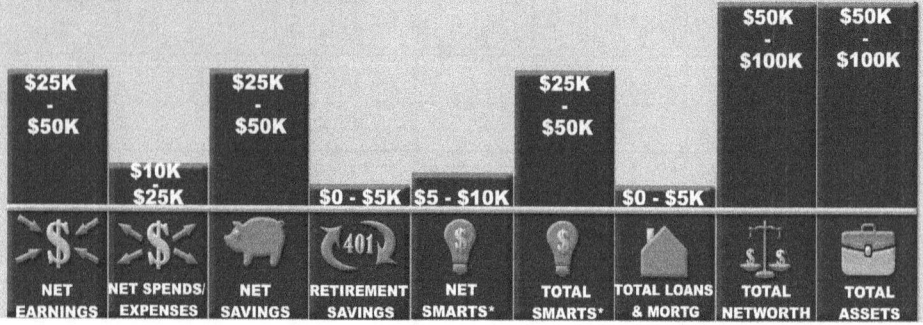

Year	2002
Net Earnings	$25,000 - $50,000
Yearly Net Spending & Investment	$10,000 - $25,000
Yearly Net Savings	$25,000 - $50,000
Yearly Retirement Savings	$0 - $5,000
Yearly Smart Savings	$5,000 - $10,000
Total Smart Savings	$25,000 - $50,000
Total Loans & Mortgages	$0 - $5,000
Total Net Worth	$50,000 - $100,000
Total Assets	$50,000 - $100,000

PERSONAL INSIGHTS:

44

2003

Don't stretch yourself too much with a mortgage. Buy within your means... it's not worth the sleepless nights.
- Sarah Beeny

Initial few months of this year were extremely hectic at the client site—even though I was selected for a longer-term assignment, I still did not consider myself an expert in the new skills. So I continued working around the clock to ensure my then-limited skills limitation did not become the roadblock in my progress. Eventually, I became so adept with the new programs that I volunteered to provide internal training and resources to those who needed it or were interested in learning more. This gesture was well-received by my company and placed me in a more positive light and was helpful in negotiations for a pay raise.

Now that I was a little more familiar with the surrounding areas, my weekend leisure activities included taking road trips to see Niagara Falls, Cape Cod and other places close by. I chose ground travel for these trips because it was both cost-effective and gave me more flexibility, and because I had still not overcome my fear of flying. Unfortunately, a hidden cost of these trips ended up being my speeding tickets—I got to more and started to run very high on points. I called the DMV and asked how I could reduce these points. The solution: taking an aggressive driving class. Though the classes were long and not necessarily that interesting, it was more important for me to have a lower insurance rate.

This year my mother visited me the very first time in the United

States. I had not gone back to India in nearly three years, so it was good to see some family again and it was great to have hot, home cooked food daily! At certain point in the year, I was the only person left in the apartment due to both of my roommates finding projects outside of Virginia. They both moved out right around the time my mother was visiting, so I did not bother to find new roommates. My monthly expenses started to go up at this time as well, since I had virtually no more shared expenses. This made me start thinking that I might be better off owning a home instead of renting since I felt that I would probably settle down in this area anyway.

I started my search for my first home in the Herndon area. I reached out to a couple of realtors and explored with few different properties, but nothing really clicked or caught my attention. I half-heartedly settled on one place and almost placed the initial deposit, but pulled back on my offer before I did because I knew it was not the place for me. I finally found the realtor who understood my needs well and found something for me that I wanted to buy. I had several things in mind when I was looking at homes: I wanted a new home that would be ready within three to six months, preferably a townhouse under $350,000 (this was the number I came up with after doing some math; the highest I could go without taking out a second mortgage). I wanted the home in a low-risk area in Fairfax County (where there would be little market fluctuation and where I knew I could rent it easily should I need to move out of town again for a project). Ideally, it would have two levels of AC management (which saves on gas and electricity in the long run) and have it face east or west (for more daylight). I also wanted something within a 15-mile radius of my worksite. I found something matching these specifications and signed off on it—the first of many amazing feelings I had in my journey to own a home.

One of the most important things for me was to one more thing I should be able to get good mortgage rate, so one of the tasks for my realtor was to find me the best mortgage rate provider. This was a worthwhile exercise that helped me find a rate that was nearly 1.75% less than what my homebuilder's company was quoting. Though they offered a competitive closing cost benefit, the mortgage rate is what really makes a difference when it comes to saving money—we do a simple math on the amortization for a $300,000 loan, a difference of 1.75% translates into nearly $100,000 in interest savings on a 30 year mortgage.

Finding a competitive mortgage rate requires having very good credit, however. Here are some things I have learned throughout the years about building—and maintaining—a good credit score.

Credit Score Tips

Within a year or so of me being in the States, I started to pay off my credit card bill at a slightly higher amount than what was actually billed. This worked to my benefit because the bank waived any late fees the couple of times that I missed a timely payment. If possible, enable online bill payment. When I did this, I started making multiple payments each month and just stopped waiting for my monthly bill to arrive. This approach helped me be more in tune with my finances and helped me never be late on a payment again. If possible, turn on auto payments for your utilities—these are bills that must be paid, and must be paid on time, so why not save yourself the worry and have the money taken out on time each month? (If you do use auto-pay, be sure to keep an eye on the bills regardless—you never know where there might be a human or computer error.)

I also tried to pay with a credit card whenever I could because it helps build your credit. I had a primary credit card for mainstream in-store and online purchases and I keep a secondary credit card with a low credit limit for non-mainstream online plus offline stores. Additionally, I had a rewards point system linked to my credit card so it helped me to earn lots of points! Some people are wary of credit cards, but as I learned from some of my friends, having no credit is just as bad as having poor credit or disputed credit. With that said, try to stay away having too many credit card—an average of two or three cards are more than enough to build your credit as long as you are building credit via auto loans and mortgage loans in the long run. It also becomes harder to manage your finances when you have too many credit cards. And although there is no harm in signing for a new credit card offered by a store if you are really getting a huge discount on your purchase, I would recommend to close on the card once you are done with the purchase and do not make any other purchases for a while through that store. (This can be tricky—because you should not be opening credit cards for minor purchase discounts; opening and closing credit cards frequently may negatively impact your credit scores.) Lastly, as much as possible, I tried to consolidate my credit to my primary credit company. So in certain instances, I paid to my other credit card company using my primary credit card checks.

I have compiled these tips into a handy reference guide at the back of the book (Credit Score Tips) so you may turn to them whenever you need.

One fine day, when I had time for myself, I was sitting in my room and started to think that it was almost five years that I moved to the USA. I initially thought of earning over $100K in savings within three years and return to India. This never really happened because not everyone gets everything from life that they want and nothing comes free or easy! So here I had already spent five years in the USA, I was moving toward a new outlook in life. It was at this time that I started dreaming of becoming a millionaire. I do not know why I had this thought or where it came from, but it became my goal in life.

Financial Insights:

Got commited to buying a new home. Spendings involves over $10,000 in just the deposit that I made for booking my new home. After almost 4 long years in the US, this was the year when I crossed my net earnings over $50,000 mark. My decision in 2002, of putting my efforts in learning new technologies worked into my favor resulting into some noticeable raise in my salary and bonus structure in this year. Also, this is the year to mark when I crossed $100,000 mark in my assets and networth.

This year I achieved smart savings of almost $10,000, which brought my total amount for smart savings for the past five years to $50,000. This was the first time I began to see the larger impact of my smarts saving method, as my net worth and assets crossed the $100,000 mark this year.

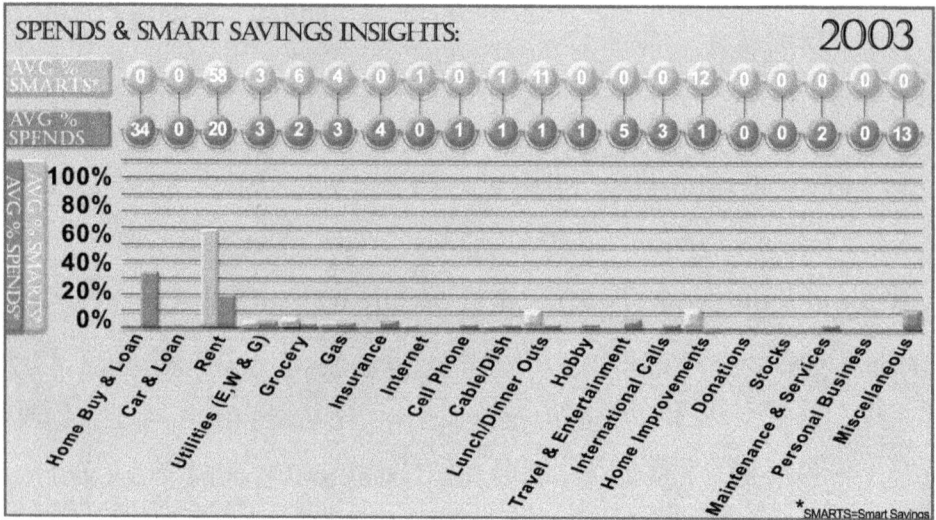

SPENDS & SMART SAVINGS INSIGHTS: 2003

	Home Buy & Loan	Car & Loan	Rent	Utilities (E, W & G)	Grocery	Gas	Insurance	Internet	Cell Phone	Cable/Dish	Lunch/Dinner Outs	Travel & Entertainment	Hobby	International Calls	Home Improvements	Donations	Stocks	Maintenance & Services	Personal Business	Miscellaneous
AVG % SMARTS*	0	0	58	3	6	4	0	1	0	1	11	0	0	0	12	0	0	0	0	0
AVG % SPENDS	34	0	20	3	2	3	4	0	1	1	1	1	5	3	1	0	0	2	0	13

*SMARTS=Smart Savings

Expense Categories	Spending	SmartS $	SmartS %	Notes
Home Buy & Loan	34.5%	-	0.0%	New Home Deposit
Car Buy & Loan	0.0%	-	0.0%	
Rent	20.7%	5,800	58.5%	+$: Shared Rent
Utilities (E,W & G)	3.3%	360	3.6%	+$: Shared, Usage conscious
Grocery	2.6%	600	6.0%	+$: Shared
Gas	3.3%	480	4.8%	+$: Accommodation near client site
Insurance	4.0%	-	0.0%	
Internet	0.6%	150	1.5%	+$: Shared
Cell Phone	1.7%	-	0.0%	+$: Group Deal, Contract
Cable/Dish	1.0%	180	1.8%	+$: Shared
Lunch/Dinner Outs	1.2%	1,152	11.6%	+$: Cooking home
Hobby	1.2%	-	0.0%	
Travel & Entertainment	5.2%	-	0.0%	+$: Group Deals, Group Travel
International Calls	3.3%	-	0.0%	
Home Improvements	1.4%	1,200	12.1%	+$: Limited necessity furniture ONLY
Donations	0.2%	-	0.0%	
Stocks	0.0%	-	0.0%	
Maintenance & Services	2.1%	-	0.0%	
Personal Business	0.0%	-	0.0%	
Miscellaneous	13.8%	-	0.0%	Includes expenses for Dependants
Total	100.0%	9,922	100.0%	

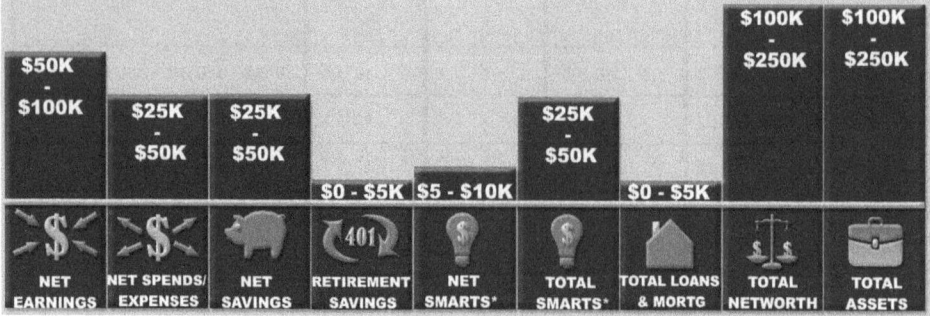

$50K - $100K	$25K - $50K	$25K - $50K	$0 - $5K	$5 - $10K	$25K - $50K	$0 - $5K	$100K - $250K	$100K - $250K
NET EARNINGS	NET SPENDS/ EXPENSES	NET SAVINGS	RETIREMENT SAVINGS	NET SMARTS*	TOTAL SMARTS*	TOTAL LOANS & MORTG	TOTAL NETWORTH	TOTAL ASSETS

Year	2003
Net Earnings	$50,000 - $100,000
Yearly Net Spending & Investment	$25,000 - $50,000
Yearly Net Savings	$25,000 - $50,000
Yearly Retirement Savings	$0 - $5,000
Yearly Smart Savings	$5,000 - $10,000
Total Smart Savings	$25,000 - $50,000
Total Loans & Mortgages	$0 - $5,000
Total Net Worth	$100,000 - $250,000
Total Assets	$100,000 - $250,000

PERSONAL INSIGHTS:

EXCELLENT
VERY GOOD
GOOD
FAIR
POOR

HEALTH   FITNESS   SOCIAL   CHARITY   HAPPINESS

2004

If you consistently spend less than you make, then the need to borrow money should be both temporary and relatively rare.
- Jeff Yeager

After almost a year of waiting, 2004 greeted me with some good news—I received my Green Card! It was a significant moment because it was a step forward to being free to work anywhere in the US without the need for an employer-sponsored visa. There is a certain duality in life that brings happiness with sadness, excitement with anxiety, and success with downfalls. So even though I was celebrating the arrival of my Green Card, negotiations did not go well between my employer and my client. However, this time around I was less anxious about finding a new project because of my newly broadened employment options. I knew that I now had the option of searching for work outside of my company, and this (and the fact that I parted my company on good terms) brought me some relief. At this time, I accepted an offer from my client and moved on to a new phase of my professional career into an entry level technology management role.

In late May, the home that I settled on was almost getting ready. I was excited and anxious as the closing date approached and I made the arrangements for the down payment and monthly mortgage. Though I was going to pay more per month in my mortgage than I would if I had rented, I was now paying to own something, thus making the payments in my favor that helped me build on my asset.

I was aggressively trying to get the best possible mortgage rate and found that if I could manage a 20% down payment, I would be able to get a great locked rate of 4.25% from one of the mortgage companies. This was pretty significant and a great rate I believe for a first time buyer in 2004. I went ahead with it. In doing my mortgage research, I learned that making biweekly (as opposed to monthly) payments saves more on interest in the long run as the mortgage can be paid off faster. It is also good to go for an added principal whenever you can, as it can also lower your long-term interest. Last, weight your options about a 30-year fixed mortgage or a 5-year ARM.

On June 23, I moved into my very first home in the US. Again, it is a feeling that I cannot quite describe, but one that is both fulfilling and unforgettable. It was another milestone in my journey and another point in establishing my life in this country.

So I moved in and looked around and realized that my new house was very empty. I was ready to settle down and make this home more permanent, so I was willing to spend some more on furniture, electronics and decorations. While the home was being prepared, I had made a mental list of some items that I definitely needed: a washing machine and dryer; televisions for both levels; a couple of fans to help with air conditioning costs; a nice dining table; two sofa sets (one for everyday use and another more luxurious set); and of course, kitchenware.

Financial Insights:

My major spending was related to a very high down payment for my new home purchase. This surely helped in generating a significant amount of smart savings as I did not have to take second loan and was able to lockin a better rate.

While I generated over $30,000 in smart savings primarily due to a very high down payment for my home purchase, I lost some potential smart savings because I made the decision to live on my own this year. Though living with roommates saved me money and was a good experience, I wanted more privacy and independence at this point in my life, which is why I purchased my own home.

My total assets reached almost $500,000 due to owning a home, but my net worth was still in the $100,000 - $250,000 range because I took out almost $300,000 a loan for my new home.

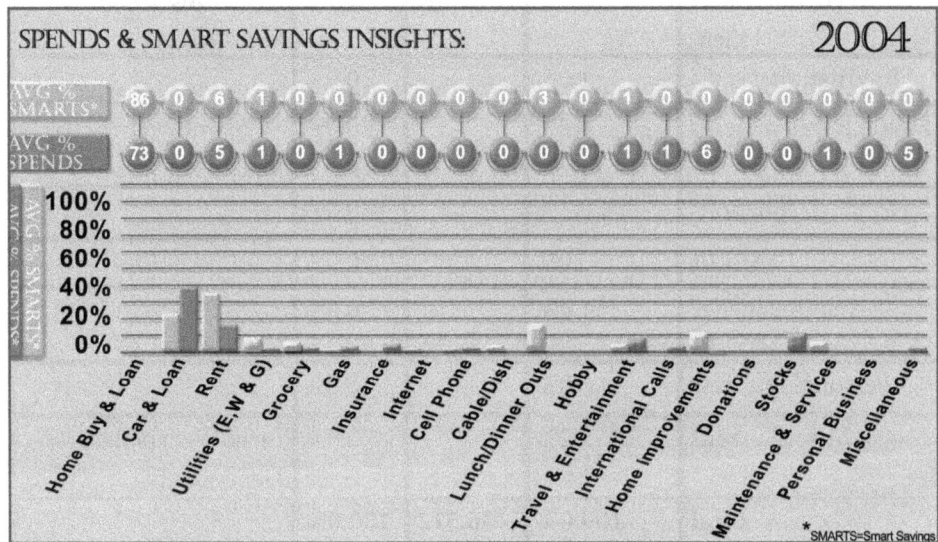

SPENDS & SMART SAVINGS INSIGHTS: 2004

AVG % SMARTS*: 86 0 6 1 0 0 0 0 0 0 3 0 1 0 0 0 0 0 0 0

AVG % SPENDS: 73 0 5 1 0 1 0 0 0 0 0 0 1 1 6 0 0 1 0 5

100% 80% 60% 40% 20% 0%

Home Buy & Loan, Car & Loan, Rent, Utilities (E,W & G), Grocery, Gas, Insurance, Internet, Cell Phone, Cable/Dish, Lunch/Dinner Outs, Hobby, Travel & Entertainment, International Calls, Home Improvements, Donations, Stocks, Maintenance & Services, Personal Business, Miscellaneous

*SMARTS=Smart Savings

Expense Categories	Spending	SmartS $	SmartS %	Notes
Home Buy & Loan	73.4%	32,000	87.6%	+$: High down payment, Negotiated mortgage rate
Car Buy & Loan	0.0%	-	0.0%	
Rent	5.6%	2,400	6.6%	+$: NOT shared but small decent apartment
Utilities (E,W & G)	1.0%	360	1.0%	+$: Shared, Usage conscious
Grocery	0.8%	-	0.0%	
Gas	1.0%	200	0.5%	+$: Accomodation near client site
Insurance	1.2%	-	0.0%	
Internet	0.2%	-	0.0%	
Cell Phone	0.5%	-	0.0%	
Cable/Dish	0.3%	-	0.0%	
Lunch/Dinner Outs	0.3%	1,152	3.2%	+$: Cooking home
Hobby	0.4%	-	0.0%	
Travel & Entertainment	1.2%	400	1.1%	+$: Group Deals, Group Travel
International Calls	1.0%	-	0.0%	
Home Improvements	6.2%	-	0.0%	-$: Spent over 3K in luxury big screen TV
Donations	0.1%	-	0.0%	
Stocks	0.0%	-	0.0%	
Maintenance & Services	1.6%	-	0.0%	
Personal Business	0.0%	-	0.0%	
Miscellaneous	5.2%	-	0.0%	Includes expenses for Dependants
Total	100.0%	36,512	100.0%	

FINANCIAL INSIGHTS:

Year	2004
Net Earnings	$50,000 - $100,000
Yearly Net Spending & Investment	$50,000 - $100,000
Yearly Net Savings	$0 - $5,000
Yearly Retirement Savings	$5,000 - $10,000
Yearly Smart Savings	$25,000 - $50,000
Total Smart Savings	$50,000 - $100,000
Total Loans & Mortgages	$250,000 - $500,000
Total Net Worth	$100,000 - $250,000
Total Assets	$250,000 - $500,000

PERSONAL INSIGHTS:

57

2005

A bargain ain't a bargain unless it's something you need.

- Sidney Carroll

As I was settling into my new home, I took an interest in decorating it and buying new things to fill the space. However, I found myself having to hold back on buying new wares before I became too extravagant in my purchases. I made myself become a window shopper for a while—whenever I was tempted to buy something new for the house, I would look at it, check the price, and add it to the list of things I wanted. If I still wanted it after going home and thinking about it, and I was still inclined to buy it when I visited the store a second time, then and only then did I actually make the purchase. It was an effective way to suppress my impulse buying behavior. Impulse buying accounts for a lot of sales, for we act with our emotions at times and not necessarily with our heads—but there are ways to cut down on this behavior and save money. Below I've outlined some tips that worked for me.

Impulse Buying Tips

Oftentimes when I bought something, I went home to realize that I did not get the best deal or the best product for the price. As with mortgages, car loans and credit cards, do your research about anything you want to purchase. It will not only save you a trip to return items, but lots of time and money as well. Along the same lines, some of my impulse purchases ended up sitting around or were just left unused. This made me feel guilty about spending the money in the first place. Sometimes I would pass off the item to a friend or sell it at a lower price, but that is not possible with everything. Also, I saw that I was more likely to spend if I was out shopping with friends who were extravagant shoppers. I would end up visiting more stores and buy things that I never really needed.

Aside from home goods, I would make a lot of impulse purchases while grocery shopping. When I did not use these products, they would go bad and I would have to throw them away, which would make me feel bad that I wasted money and food! I realized that most of my impulse food purchases were because I went shopping when I was hungry or thirsty. I would buy food or drinks that were on sale that week or just because they were in front of me. I found that making a list—whether in my head, on paper, or in my phone—helped me cut back substantially on unnecessary purchases. I would not feel the need to browse every aisle aimlessly, but would only go after the items I knew I wanted. Overall, I was more likely to purchase both food and non-food items if I went shopping while I was in a bad mood. It seemed that these impulse purchases brought me temporary joy. Remember, impulse buying brings short-term joy, but planning brings long-term joy—and financial freedom!

Keep in mind that impulse buying is not limited to just in-store purchases. In today's Internet world, knowingly or unknowingly, we subscribe to so many newsletters and catalogs and alerts that are delivered to our inbox each day. If you find yourself tempted by these offers, take the time to unsubscribe from some of them and just keep the ones that are truly valuable. This reduces temptation and also the time it takes to read through everything each day. Remember that deals and discounts are like buses—there is a pattern to them and they are always coming and going.

This year I finished my first year at my new job and got a decent salary increase and a bonus. I immediately deposited my bonus and wrote out a check to my mortgage company for that exact amount. Though it did not change my monthly total, this still helped reduce the amount of interest that I had to keep paying to my mortgage company, and with that, increased my principal paid as part of each mortgage payment. To give further more perspective of what I am describing, here is a chart that shows the value of smart savings related to additional principal on loans:

Mort-gage Amount	In-terest Rate	Term	Added Principal Monthly	Final Payoff	Total Interest	Your Smart
$300,000	6.25%	30 Years	$0	30 Years	$364,975	$0
$300,000	6.25%	30 Years	$100	26 Years	$307,887	$57,088
$300,000	6.25%	30 Years	$200	23 Years	$267,775	$97,200
$300,000	6.25%	30 Years	$300	21 Years	$237,689	$127,286
$300,000	6.25%	30 Years	$400	19 Years	$214,120	$150,855
$300,000	6.25%	30 Years	$500	17 Years	$195,073	$169,902
$300,000	6.25%	30 Years	$1,000	12 Years	$136,176	$228,799

As you can see, just by adding $100 to the monthly principal, you can save almost $57,000 in interest. As you increase by another hundred, your incremental savings almost multiply. As I was doing the above, I thought why not to add the savings I generate from my tax savings because of the mortgage interest paid. So adding that into the mix, I came up with these numbers:

Mortgage Amount	Interest Rate	Term	Added Principal Monthly	Final Payoff	Total Interest (By Term End)	Tax Saving	Net Interest Paid	Your Smart Savings
$300,000	6.25%	30 Years	$0	30 Years	$364,975	$91,244	$273,731	$0
$300,000	6.25%	30 Years	$100	26 Years	$307,887	$76,972	$230,915	$42,816
$300,000	6.25%	30 Years	$200	23 Years	$267,775	$66,944	$200,831	$72,900
$300,000	6.25%	30 Years	$300	21 Years	$237,689	$59,422	$178,267	$95,464
$300,000	6.25%	30 Years	$400	19 Years	$214,120	$53,530	$160,590	$113,141
$300,000	6.25%	30 Years	$500	17 Years	$195,073	$48,768	$146,305	$127,426
$300,000	6.25%	30 Years	$1,000	12 Years	$136,176	$34,044	$102,132	$171,599

Although it looks very enticing to get some money back in form of tax savings due to mortgage interest at the end of every year, it's still not as much as you would gain in the long run just adding $100 monthly to your mortgage payment in form of added principal.

This is just my way of looking at things; one can always argue different routes to take, such as using the money in hand to invest into something that can bring more. But that goes into an altogether different business and risk-taking approach. My focus is for those who are not big risk takers and prefer putting their eggs in several baskets at a higher risk versus spreading our eggs in few baskets at a lower risk!

Moving on from mortgages and interest—this year I had to attend defensive driving classes for a day to reduce on the points on my license that I had accumulated due to a high number of speeding tickets. While it helped me reduce my points, it did not help lower my auto insurance! I feel this is worth mentioning because tickets are not necessarily a one-time fee. There are residual effects associated with them, such as increased auto insurance payments (for three to five years), taking the time to take these classes, and dealing with points on your license.

Financial Insights:

As you notice there was a major dip in my smart savings primarily attributed to me moving into my own home with no more shared costs in the key expense areas. However, I still managed to keep a decent chunk in my smart savings primarily by making added principal payments on my mortgage, resulting in a gradual reduction in interest.

The biggest contributor to my smart savings this year was the added principal to my mortgage payments, which saved me from paying a lot of interest over time. I also made sure to reel in my impulsive buying when it came to purchases for my new home!

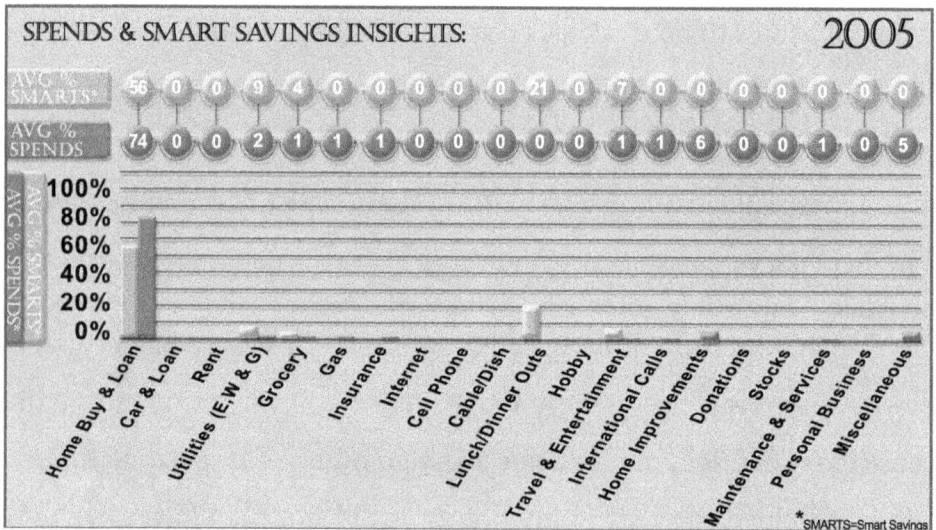

SPENDS & SMART SAVINGS INSIGHTS:																			2005
AVG % SMARTS*	56	0	0	9	4	0	0	0	0	0	21	0	7	0	0	0	0	0	0	0
AVG % SPENDS	74	0	0	2	1	1	1	0	0	0	0	0	1	1	6	0	0	1	0	5

Categories: Home Buy & Loan, Car & Loan, Rent, Utilities (E, W & G), Grocery, Gas, Insurance, Internet, Cell Phone, Cable/Dish, Lunch/Dinner Outs, Hobby, Travel & Entertainment, International Calls, Home Improvements, Donations, Stocks, Maintenance & Services, Personal Business, Miscellaneous

AVG % SPENDS scale: 100%, 80%, 60%, 40%, 20%, 0%

*SMARTS=Smart Savings

Expense Categories	Spend-ing	SmartS $	SmartS %	Notes
Home Buy & Loan	74.1%	3,000	56.9%	$+: Loan Payment + Added Principal to reduce Interest $s
Car Buy & Loan	0.0%	-	0.0%	
Rent	0.0%	-	0.0%	
Utilities (E,W & G)	2.4%	480	9.1%	+$: Usage conscious
Grocery	1.7%	240	4.6%	+$: Shopping when NOT hungry, NOT thirsty
Gas	1.1%		0.0%	
Insurance	1.3%	-	0.0%	-$: Multiple Speeding Tickets
Internet	0.6%	-	0.0%	
Cell Phone	0.6%	-	0.0%	
Cable/Dish	0.6%	-	0.0%	
Lunch/Dinner Outs	0.4%	1,152	21.9%	+$: Cooking home
Hobby	0.4%	-	0.0%	
Travel & Entertainment	1.4%	400	7.6%	+$: Group Deals, Group Travel
International Calls	1.1%	-	0.0%	
Home Improve-ments	6.9%	-	0.0%	
Donations	0.2%	-	0.0%	
Stocks	0.0%	-	0.0%	
Maintenance & Services	1.7%	-	0.0%	
Personal Business	0.0%	-	0.0%	
Miscellaneous	5.7%	-	0.0%	Includes expenses for Dependants
Total	100.0%	5,272	100.0%	

								$250K - $500K
						$100K - $250K	$100K - $250K	
$50K - $100K	$50K - $100K				$50K - $100K			
			$10K - $25K					
		$5 - $10K		$5 - $10K				
NET EARNINGS	NET SPENDS/ EXPENSES	NET SAVINGS	RETIREMENT SAVINGS	NET SMARTS*	TOTAL SMARTS*	TOTAL LOANS & MORTG	TOTAL NETWORTH	TOTAL ASSETS

Year	2005
Net Earnings	$50,000 - $100,000
Yearly Net Spending & Investment	$50,000 - $100,000
Yearly Net Savings	$5,000 - $10,000
Yearly Retirement Savings	$10,000 - $25,000
Yearly Smart Savings	$5,000 - $10,000
Total Smart Savings	$50,000 - $100,000
Total Loans & Mortgages	$100,000 - $250,000
Total Net Worth	$100,000 - $250,000
Total Assets	$250,000 - $500,000

PERSONAL INSIGHTS:

EXCELLENT
VERY GOOD
GOOD
FAIR
POOR

| HEALTH | FITNESS | SOCIAL | CHARITY | HAPPINESS |

2006

I have learnt to seek my happiness in limiting my desires, rather than attempting to satisfy them.

- John Stuart Mill

By this year I had completed two years at my new job and was happy to get another raise and another bonus. Just as I did last year, I wrote a check in the amount of my bonus to my mortgage company towards my principal to help me further reduce on the interest amount paid.

As much as I tried to stay on top of things, there are certain events that cannot be prevented (or predicted, for that matter). One morning in late March, I was sitting behind a red light on my way to work and saw a car barreling down the road right behind me with no intention of stopping. My immediate reaction was to turn the wheel and get off the road, but by the time I actually processed what was happening, the car hit me from behind. Despite breaking to avoid veering off the road, I still lost control and thankfully stopped short of hitting some trees. As soon as the initial shock wore off and I tried to drive my car to the side of the road, I realized that the rear was dragging on the asphalt and that the car was no long in drivable condition. The car was totaled, and aside from some minor back pain, I avoided injury—or so I thought.

Throughout the day, my pain intensified to the point where I had to take a couple of days off work just to rest. After X-rays, an MRI and several visits to a specialist, it was determined that I had a disc protrusion that was putting pressure on some nerves which caused some lower leg pain as well. This affected both my work and personal life. I spent some time in pursuit of returning to a life without pain. Doctors advised against surgery for my case, so I was visiting various chiropractors to help me out. I even took a trip to India during this period to seek some treatment with a famed chiropractor, which ended up being the most useful therapy.

MENTION: This year I started getting thoughts around starting my own business venture. I started thinking of few concepts and ideas but my accident prevented me from pursuing my thoughts around business.

Before I knew it, I was back in the auto market looking for a new car to replace my totaled car. With the money I received from my insurance company, I set out to purchase a new car. Even though I received less money from insurance than I had hoped, I decided to go for a little upgrade. My criteria were still largely the same, even though this time around I debated buying a hybrid car as well. At that time, the benefits of the hybrid were outweighed by the fact that it cost about $5,000 more, so I decided against it. I settled on a new, top of the line Honda Accord.

I received some more disappointing news as we were working out a loan deal and they conducted a credit check. They told me that the check did not go well and I could not get the interest rate that I had been hoping to get—and instead had to get one that was nearly 2.5% more. I was surprised to hear this, as I knew that I had built up good credit with my bills and mortgage payments, but was even more surprised to hear the reason that my credit was not as good as it used to be. It turns out that there was an unsettled payment conflict for $150 with my mobile service provider. I recalled that I though was being unfairly billed, so I did not agree to make the payment. However, my mobile service provider sent this bill to a collections agency, and this dispute ended up harming my credit score. Again, it was very disheartening to know that such a small sum had a large impact on both my score and the interest rate on a loan.

In the end, I made a calculated decision to not go with a loan. However, I did not have enough in my bank account at the time to write a single check for the car. I asked the auto dealership to lock on the offer and I would be back next day with a check (after I had made some transfers from my savings account) to pay off the car in a single payment.

This resulted in an upfront smart savings in the amount of $5,000+ for me, by paying in full! Here is my simple math:

Loan Amount	Loan Rate	Loan Term	SmartS	Notes
$25,000	7.85%	5 years	$5,000+	$+: No Auto Loan Interest $s payments savings

Running through the amortization calculator, by the end of 60 months, I would have paid over $5,000 in interest if I had kept all my savings in the bank and not used it for paying off on my purchase. Though I fell short on my emergency cash flow, I decided to take this risk in order to not take out a loan.

I realized that this would set me back on my added principal payment for my mortgage, but after doing the math, I determined that I was better off taking my savings and paying off my car in full. Before I wrap up my second auto buying experience, I thought to share a tips on how to save money when car shopping.

Auto Buying Tips

It is very easy to get carried away when purchasing a car. Because it is something that we will be sitting in and driving daily, it becomes easy to rationalize features that are not necessary, but mainly for enjoyment. I would recommend that an auto loan be less than or equal to 5% of your monthly earnings. Do your homework online and research the type of car you want before you land at a dealership. Even better, visit multiple dealerships because cars come in and go out faster than they are listed online. When you are at the dealership, do not hesitate to bargain. They are prepared to bargain with you, so drive a hard deal and see what you can get out of it. See what is important to you and use that as your bargaining platform—financing for a certain number of months, a direct discount on the total price, some added feature or discount, etc. When it comes to loans, talk to different dealerships and see who is offering the best option (such as 0% interest rates).

Financial Insights:

As you notice, my major area of spending is focused towards paying my mortgage and constantly adding more towards principal but was not enough this year due to me buying new car in full payment with no loan. New car buying was an unexpected expense due to my old car getting totaled during my accident. Also, another important note of mention, I controlled on my impulses towards filling up every corner of my house with furniture and stayed focused on my necessities first keeping my home improvement budget under good check.

This year my total assets crossed the $500,000 mark as my home value kept going up. As in the previous year, I invested the maximum amount in my retirement fund as I was determined to build up that fund as much as possible.

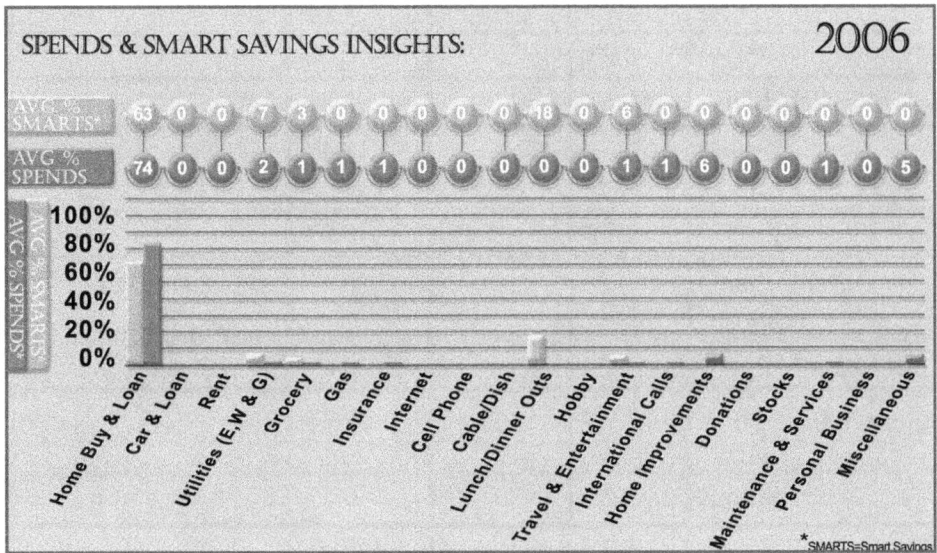

SPENDS & SMART SAVINGS INSIGHTS: 2006

	Home Buy & Loan	Car & Loan	Rent	Utilities (E, W & G)	Grocery	Gas	Insurance	Internet	Cell Phone	Cable/Dish	Lunch/Dinner Outs	Hobby	Travel & Entertainment	International Calls	Home Improvements	Donations	Stocks	Maintenance & Services	Personal Business	Miscellaneous
AVG % SMARTS*	63	0	0	7	3	0	0	0	0	18	0	6	0	0	0	0	0	0		
AVG % SPENDS	74	0	0	2	1	1	0	0	0	0	0	1	1	6	0	0	1	0	5	

AVG % SMARTS / AVG % SPENDS: 100% 80% 60% 40% 20% 0%

*SMARTS=Smart Savings

Expense Categories	Spending	SmartS $	SmartS %	Notes
Home Buy & Loan	58.0%	4,000	63.8%	$+: Loan Payment + Added Principal to reduce Interest $s
Car Buy & Loan	22.0%	5,000	0.0%	
Rent	0.0%	-	0.0%	
Utilities (E,W & G)	2.0%	480	7.7%	+$: Usage conscious
Grocery	1.0%	240	3.8%	+$: Shopping when NOT hungry, NOT thirsty
Gas	1.0%		0.0%	
Insurance	1.3%	-	0.0%	
Internet	0.6%	-	0.0%	
Cell Phone	0.6%	-	0.0%	
Cable/Dish	0.6%	-	0.0%	
Lunch/Dinner Outs	0.3%	1,152	18.4%	+$: Cooking home
Hobby	0.2%	-	0.0%	
Travel & Entertainment	1.4%	400	6.4%	+$: Group Deals, Group Travel
International Calls	1.1%	-	0.0%	
Home Improvements	5.0%	-	0.0%	
Donations	0.2%	-	0.0%	
Stocks	0.0%	-	0.0%	
Maintenance & Services	1.7%	-	0.0%	
Personal Business	0.0%	-	0.0%	
Miscellaneous	4.1%	-	0.0%	Includes expenses for Dependants
Total	100.0%	6,272	100.0%	

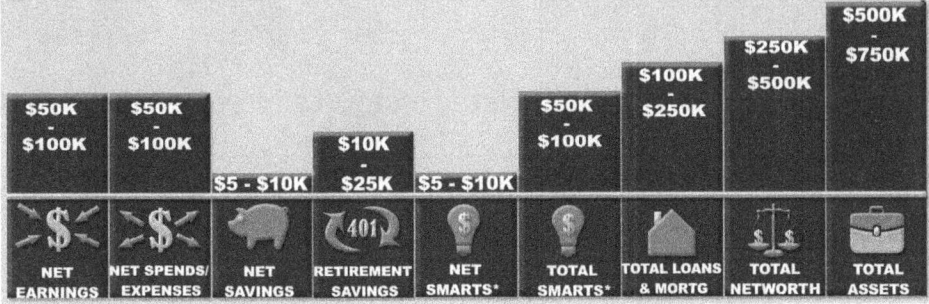

Year	2006
Net Earnings	$50,000 - $100,000
Yearly Net Spending & Investment	$50,000 - $100,000
Yearly Net Savings	$5,000 - $10,000
Yearly Retirement Savings	$10,000 - $25,000
Yearly Smart Savings	$5,000 - $10,000
Total Smart Savings	$50,000 - $100,000
Total Loans & Mortgages	$100,000 - $250,000
Total Net Worth	$250,000 - $500,000
Total Assets	$500,000 - $750,000

PERSONAL INSIGHTS:

71

2007

The darkest day in a man's career is that wherein he fancies there is some easier way of getting a dollar than by squarely earning it.

- Horace Greeley

This year started with my search for a lawyer following my car accident. I talked to a few friends, but most did not know what the next step should be. I found out later that I could have reached out to my employer's free consultation and legal services. Be sure to know your options and explore your resources that your employer provides (if they provide any)—they can save you a lot of legal fees if you consult with them first.

I completed my third year at this job and was promoted to Senior Development Manager. I was very pleased about this, especially after the hard year of pain I endured. I was also happy to see that despite circumstances that took me away from my work for a while, they were still pleased enough to promote me.

Around June, I decided to register the company name for my business venture, since the idea never really left my head. Some say it is more vital to have an idea first and work through that before registering the name, but it was a practical decision for me because it allowed me to track the expenses associated with this venture. Between my day job and the nights I spent working on this, the rest of this year flew by. I assembled a small team in India to work with me, and would stay up until 1 am or 2 am so I could communicate with them. Still, my priority was my day job and I made sure that none of this side business impacted my performance at work.

MENTION: Initially, I used to do my own taxes because they were not very involved and I could get by easily with readily available, low-cost software. However, I hired a tax consultant when I started my business and felt that I was going beyond my basic tax-filing skills. Aside from that, it is a good idea to leverage the services of a tax consultant at least once, if only to check that what you are doing on your own is correct. Sometimes tax consultants will also discover tax breaks and other exceptions for which you may not have known you were eligible.

Financial Insights:

One of the primary driver in the lift I achieved with my networth can be attributed to my house value that resulting in almost $130,000 appraised in just 4 years of my purchase. This was the first year of me seeding money into my business ideas. I kept thinking to myself how much I should invest into my business ideas to minimize my risk on failures but it was high time that I wanted to start trying out in a controlled fashion.

This year I earned $100,000 in smart savings and also crossed the $500,000 mark for my total net worth. Additionally, after eight years into my professional career in the US, my net earnings for the year finally crossed the $100,000 mark.

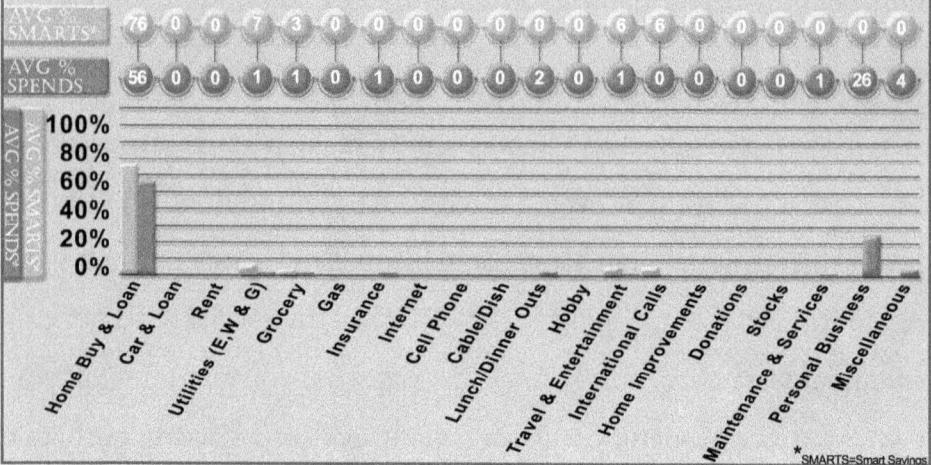

SPENDS & SMART SAVINGS INSIGHTS: 2007

	Home Buy & Loan	Car & Loan	Rent	Utilities (E,W & G)	Grocery	Gas	Insurance	Internet	Cell Phone	Cable/Dish	Lunch/Dinner Outs	Hobby	Travel & Entertainment	International Calls	Home Improvements	Donations	Stocks	Maintenance & Services	Personal Business	Miscellaneous
AVG % SMARTS*	76	0	0	7	3	0	0	0	0	0	0	0	6	6	0	0	0	0	0	0
AVG % SPENDS	56	0	0	1	1	0	1	0	0	0	2	0	1	0	0	0	0	1	26	4

*SMARTS=Smart Savings

74

Expense Categories	Spending	SmartS $	SmartS %	Notes
Home Buy & Loan	56.4%	5,000	76.7%	$+: Loan Payment + Added Principal to reduce Interest $s
Car Buy & Loan	0.0%	-	0.0%	
Rent	0.0%	-	0.0%	
Utilities (E,W & G)	1.8%	480	7.4%	+$: Usage conscious
Grocery	1.3%	240	3.7%	+$: Shopping when NOT hungry, NOT thirsty !
Gas	0.8%		0.0%	
Insurance	1.0%	-	0.0%	
Internet	0.4%	-	0.0%	
Cell Phone	0.4%	-	0.0%	
Cable/Dish	0.4%	-	0.0%	
Lunch/Dinner Outs	2.2%	-	0.0%	-$: Eating mostly out, no home cooking
Hobby	0.3%	-	0.0%	
Travel & Entertainment	1.3%	400	6.1%	+$: Group Deals, Group Travel
International Calls	0.4%	400	6.1%	+$: International Calling Deals
Home Improvements	0.9%	-	0.0%	
Donations	0.3%	-	0.0%	
Stocks	0.0%	-	0.0%	
Maintenance & Services	1.3%	-	0.0%	
Personal Business	26.2%	-	0.0%	
Miscellaneous	4.4%	-	0.0%	Includes expenses for Dependants
Total	100.0%	6,520	100.0%	

$100K - $250K	$100K - $250K	$100K - $250K	$10K - $25K	$5 - $10K	$100K - $250K	$100K - $250K	$500K - $750K	$500K - $750K
NET EARNINGS	NET SPENDS/ EXPENSES	NET SAVINGS	RETIREMENT SAVINGS	NET SMARTS*	TOTAL SMARTS*	TOTAL LOANS & MORTG	TOTAL NETWORTH	TOTAL ASSETS

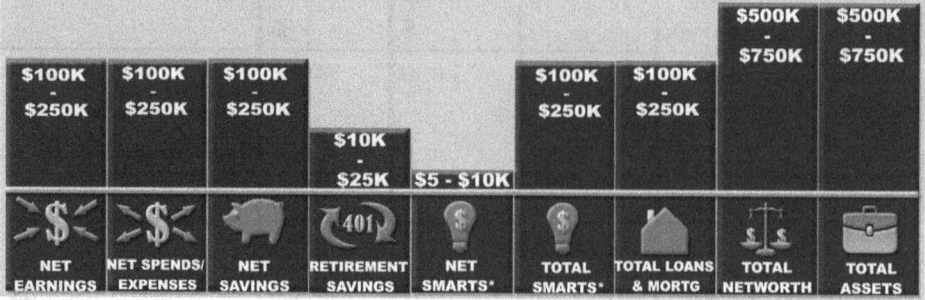

Year	2007
Net Earnings	$100,000 - $250,000
Yearly Net Spending & Investment	$100,000 - $250,000
Yearly Net Savings	$100,000 - $250,000
Yearly Retirement Savings	$10,000 - $25,000
Yearly Smart Savings	$5,000 - $10,000
Total Smart Savings	$100,000 - $250,000
Total Loans & Mortgages	$100,000 - $250,000
Total Net Worth	$500,000 - $750,000
Total Assets	$500,000 - $750,000

PERSONAL INSIGHTS:

EXCELLENT
VERY GOOD
GOOD
FAIR
POOR

HEALTH   FITNESS   SOCIAL   CHARITY   HAPPINESS

2008

> It's not debt per say that overwhelms an individual corporation
> or country. Rather it is a continuous increase in debt in
> relation to income that causes trouble.
> - Warren Buffett

This year brought another milestone for me as a US resident: I finally became a citizen of the United States of America. However, in doing so, I had to surrender my Indian citizenship. I was able to work out an Overseas Citizenship of India (OCI) so I could keep traveling back to my true roots whenever I needed to do so.

For most part of this year, I was very busy with my day job and pursuing my business idea at nights and on weekends. I was able to successfully launch my first set of websites as part of my business initiative. Needless to say, I faced lots of challenges and suffered quite a few setbacks during the launch and first phase of my idea.

Right around the end of the year, I reached a point wherein I had accumulated a decent amount in my savings. Savings account interest rates are very low when keeping money in the bank, so I began to think about more profitable options—should I just aggressively pursue my business idea in lieu of my day job? (I decided against this; though I had a large sum in savings, I did not think it was the right economic environment to do this.) Should I invest in some new property? (I decided against this as well; the market was neither bad nor good, but I did not want to deal with a new mortgage payment). Should I just sit on the savings the time being? (I did not do this either; there was no potential for growth.) In the end, I decided that if I was not going to invest it, I should just get the maximum value for it in my current situation. So I decided to pay off my entire home mortgage. It was a big decision, but after giving it some thought, I realized that it was the best use of my money. I wrote the check—the largest sum to date— and felt anxious until I received the letter from the mortgage company that stated I had paid my loan in full.

With the complete payment of the mortgage, I achieved a smart savings of $235,000+. Here is my simple math:

Loan Amount	Loan Rate	Loan Term	SmartS	Notes
$310,000	4.25%	30 years	$235,000+	$+: Full payoff of home mortgage, Interest $s payment savings

Running through the amortization calculator, at the end of 360 months, I would have paid over $235,000 in interest if I had kept all my savings in bank and not used it for paying off on my purchase. I was once again running pretty low on my emergency cash flow, but felt that this calculated risk was worth it.

MENTION: I researched the best available Certificate of Deposits (CD) options for my emergency cash flow (which I always pretended did not exist and was not available for spending). This way, the money is not just sitting aside, but constantly adding a certain amount of value. In the last 14 years, I would estimate that I earned anywhere from $5,000 to $10,000 in interest on my emergency cash fund. A little time put into research will reveal the best option for safekeeping this fund while keeping it easily accessible.

This year was also a big learning year for me. I funded a student movie and wrote and produced a few commercials for my website launch that were broadcast on Indian television channels in the US. Aside from that, this was the year that my first "Smart Savings Jar" got full and I started my second "Smart Savings Jar."

Learned the 80-20 rule of social circle. Giving 80% of my available time to my 20% of the key circle of friends and professional connections. It was my business that demanded lot of my night and weekend time, so my 80-20 rule of socializing helped me find the needed time.

Financial Insights:

This year's major spending was towards gaining my first major financial freedom from my mortgage payments. Now, I had more potential for me to invest into my business idea as there was one less thing for me to worry related to payment.

With over $125,000 in smart savings generated by paying off the entire home mortgage, my total net worth was equal to my total assets, making my net worth almost $750,000.

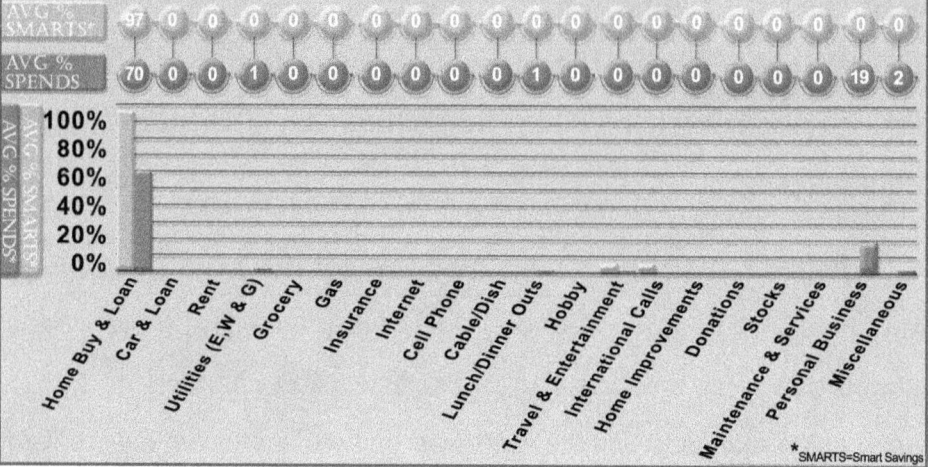

SPENDS & SMART SAVINGS INSIGHTS: 2008

AVG % SMARTS*	97	0	0	0	0	0	0	0	0	0	0	0	0	0	0	0	0	0	0	0	0
AVG % SPENDS	70	0	0	1	0	0	0	0	0	0	1	0	0	0	0	0	0	0	0	19	2

AVG % SMARTS / AVG % SPENDS

100%
80%
60%
40%
20%
0%

Home Buy & Loan, Car & Loan, Rent, Utilities (E, W & G), Grocery, Gas, Insurance, Internet, Cell Phone, Cable/Dish, Lunch/Dinner Outs, Hobby, Travel & Entertainment, International Calls, Home Improvements, Donations, Stocks, Maintenance & Services, Personal Business, Miscellaneous

*SMARTS=Smart Savings

80

Expense Categories	Spending	SmartS $	SmartS %	Notes
Home Buy & Loan	70.5%	126,000	97.8%	$+: If paid in 30 years, it would have been $200K interest
Car Buy & Loan	0.0%	-	0.0%	
Rent	0.0%	-	0.0%	
Utilities (E,W & G)	1.0%	480	0.4%	+$: Usage conscious
Grocery	0.7%	240	0.2%	+$: Shopping when NOT hungry, NOT thirsty !
Gas	0.5%	-	0.0%	
Insurance	0.6%	-	0.0%	
Internet	0.2%	-	0.0%	
Cell Phone	0.2%	-	0.0%	
Cable/Dish	0.2%	-	0.0%	
Lunch/Dinner Outs	1.6%	1,152	0.9%	+$: Cooking home
Hobby	0.2%	-	0.0%	
Travel & Entertainment	0.6%	400	0.3%	+$: Group Deals, Group Travel
International Calls	0.1%	500	0.4%	+$: International Calling Deals
Home Improvements	0.2%	-	0.0%	
Donations	0.2%	-	0.0%	
Stocks	0.0%	-	0.0%	
Maintenance & Services	0.7%	-	0.0%	
Personal Business	19.8%	-	0.0%	
Miscellaneous	2.5%	-	0.0%	Includes expenses for Dependants
Total	100.0%	128,772	100.0%	

FINANCIAL INSIGHTS:

$100K - $250K	$100K - $250K	$0 - $5K	$10K - $25K	$100K - $250K	$100K - $250K	$0 - $5K	$500K - $750K	$500K - $750K
NET EARNINGS	NET SPENDS/ EXPENSES	NET SAVINGS	RETIREMENT SAVINGS	NET SMARTS*	TOTAL SMARTS*	TOTAL LOANS & MORTG	TOTAL NETWORTH	TOTAL ASSETS

Year	2008
Net Earnings	$100,000 - $250,000
Yearly Net Spending & Investment	$100,000 - $250,000
Yearly Net Savings	$0 - $5,000
Yearly Retirement Savings	$10,000 - $25,000
Yearly Smart Savings	$100,000 - $250,000
Total Smart Savings	$100,000 - $250,000
Total Loans & Mortgages	$0 - $5,000
Total Net Worth	$500,000 - $750,000
Total Assets	$500,000 - $750,000

PERSONAL INSIGHTS:

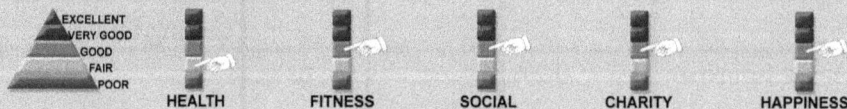

	HEALTH	FITNESS	SOCIAL	CHARITY	HAPPINESS
EXCELLENT / VERY GOOD / GOOD / FAIR / POOR					

2009

> **All days are not same. Save for a rainy day.**
> **When you don't work, savings will work for you.**
>
> - **M.K. Soni,** author

This year was quite busy at work, but due to some shifts in my group and in the organization at large, I found that I lost some of my motivation and that I was more stressed and less content with my career. I dusted off my resume and sought to find some new opportunities, both through searching via traditional avenues and also by using new websites such as LinkedIn. As I moved forward in my search, I talked to two companies and ended up getting a verbal offer from one and a very positive response from the other. At this point I explained to my boss that I felt I had become stagnant in my career and that I needed to move on to something new, but she urged me to reconsider. After talking about some changes in the workplace, I ended up staying at the company—a move that ultimately worked to my benefit, as I was (much to my surprise) promoted to Director within a few months.

I was extremely happy I decided to stay back. Even though this new role had more responsibility and a new set of challenges, it provided the momentum and motivation I needed to shed that feeling of stagnancy. As far as my own personal business ventures, things were moving slower this year. I improved the website and launched my first mobile phone application. I began to see signs of potential in my mobile application venture and continued to test different features. It was a busy time on both job fronts.

Around the middle of the year, I decided to do some cleanup around the house. I was looking around and getting the feeling that a lot of the things in my house no longer had any use for me. I went through my belongings and brought all such items to the garage to be sorted. I placed all unwanted clothing and shoes in bags to donate to a nearby charity. I cleared out obsolete or broken electronics and set them aside to be recycled, if possible (or otherwise tossed). I listed a bunch of other electronics and mechanical items that were in good working condition on eBay and Craigslist. Through this entire exercise, I generated about $1,000.

I also reached out to my cable and mobile service provider to ask if they had any discounts for long-term loyal customers. I was able to change my plan to an annual plan for the latter and get some discounts that way. Next I called my auto and home insurance companies and spoke with them on various options for coverage and deductibles. After a lengthy discussion, I made some tweaks to my coverage and asked for some additional discounts. Going into my discussions with insurance, I wanted to make sure that I did not lose coverage around liabilities and also compared the offerings of other providers before deciding to continue with my existing provider.

I think it is a good idea to do the houseclearing every year and touch base with all service providers every two years (unless something comes up that would necessitate reaching out to them sooner).

MENTION: I made sure I had a legal will created to benefit my family in case something should happen to me. It is important to me that my assets should be divided as I see fit while I have the capacity to do so. I took two-fold approach with my will. First, I did some research online and used an online services to create a quick will. Then, I followed it up with a meeting with a state attorney to finish it and submit it for records in my state. I believe it is very important for us to lay out our intentions so the people we love will receive maximum benefits. Also, when you are drawing up a will, take a look at your life insurance coverage and ensure you are doing the best for your dependants. These things might be little tough to think and may take back seat in our daily lives, but I learned from personal experience with my father's will that it makes dealing with certain issues much easier. The last thing you want is for your hard-earned money to be used in ways you never intended, and even worse, to be kept away from your loved one.

This year, I was exploring the option to further expand on my retirement planning over and beyond the regular retirement 401(k) savings. I spoke to few friends and found out that quite a few of them were leveraging services of a company with regards to managing their long term retirement planning including life insurance and low risk stock investments, mutual fund investments and more. This was a no brainer and I immediately reached out the company providing these services and decided to start investing in it at a very controlled fashion based on the guidance of this financial advisor. I burnt a bit in the past with my stock investments, so I have been staying away from stocks all this along but then I decided to go beyond mutual funds and invest in some stable stocks. One other thing, I would mention that I also invested into life insurance at this time. Key thing about this was I did not go for Term Insurance because that's provided at basic level by my company. I opted to go for Whole life Insurance, primarily because I wanted to use that in form of a retirement savings account.

I am still not sure if that was the right decision or not, I put money into it and have been seeding it. I would say that it is important to search around and see what other options are available to you beyond the standard 401(k). This is one of those areas that I do not have something solid that has already worked for me, due to age and circumstance. My research continues!

Financial Insights:

One of my friends bought a Jeep for himself and I went for ride with him couple of times. I love to drive Jeep and would find opportunities to rent it when on vacation. He tempted me enough for me to go for my second vehicle but right at the last minute, I changed my mind convincing myself to invest that money into my business venture and make further attempts to see it cross breakeven and run successfully. I told to myself whenever I feel like driving Jeep, I will just rent one for a weekend. If I had bought the Jeep it would have been one major impulse purchase!

Although I was free of mortgages and loans this year, I only achieved about $2,000 in smarts savings. This was the lowest amount I had ever saved. Most of my money went into my direct savings or into my business this year.

SPENDS & SMART SAVINGS INSIGHTS: 2009

| AVG % SMARTS* | 0 | 0 | 0 | 25 | 12 | 0 | 0 | 0 | 0 | 0 | 0 | 0 | 20 | 41 | 0 | 0 | 0 | 0 | 0 | 0 |
| AVG % SPENDS | 0 | 0 | 0 | 3 | 2 | 1 | 0 | 1 | 0 | 0 | 0 | 5 | 0 | 1 | 0 | 0 | 1 | 0 | 2 | 71 | 7 |

AVG % SMARTS

100%
80%
60%
40%
20%
0%

Home Buy & Loan · Car & Loan · Rent · Utilities (E,W & G) · Grocery · Gas · Insurance · Internet · Cell Phone · Cable/Dish · Lunch/Dinner Outs · Hobby · Travel & Entertainment · International Calls · Home Improvements · Donations · Stocks · Maintenance & Services · Personal Business · Miscellaneous

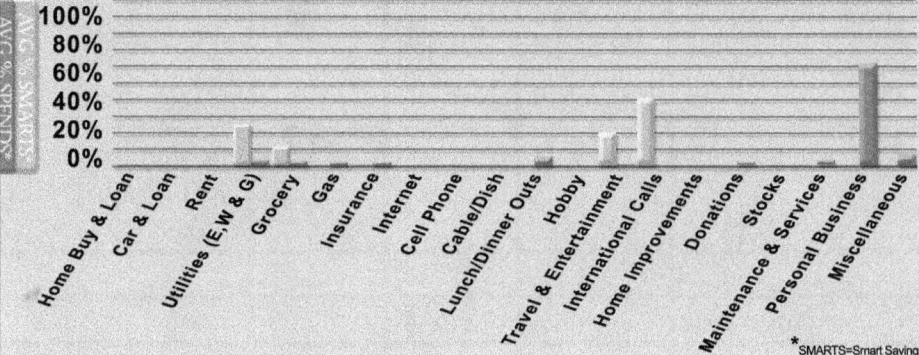

*SMARTS=Smart Savings

Expense Categories	Spending	SmartS $	SmartS %	Notes
Home Buy & Loan	0.0%	-	0.0%	
Car Buy & Loan	0.0%	-	0.0%	
Rent	0.0%	-	0.0%	
Utilities (E,W & G)	2.5%	480	42.9%	+$: Usage conscious
Grocery	1.7%	240	21.4%	+$: Shopping when NOT hungry, NOT thirsty !
Gas	1.1%	-	0.0%	
Insurance	1.4%	-	0.0%	
Internet	0.6%	-	0.0%	
Cell Phone	0.6%	-	0.0%	
Cable/Dish	0.6%	-	0.0%	
Lunch/Dinner Outs	6.5%	-	0.0%	-$: Eating mostly out, no home cooking
Hobby	0.4%	-	0.0%	
Travel & Entertainment	1.4%	400	35.7%	+$: Group Deals, Group Travel
International Calls	1.1%	-	0.0%	
Home Improvements	0.6%	-	0.0%	
Donations	1.8%	-	0.0%	
Stocks	0.0%	-	0.0%	
Maintenance & Services	1.8%	-	0.0%	
Personal Business	70.9%	-	0.0%	
Miscellaneous	7.1%	-	0.0%	Includes expenses for Dependants
Total	100.0%	1,120	100.0%	

NET EARNINGS	NET SPENDS/ EXPENSES	NET SAVINGS	RETIREMENT SAVINGS	NET SMARTS*	TOTAL SMARTS*	TOTAL LOANS & MORTG	TOTAL NETWORTH	TOTAL ASSETS
$100K - $250K	$50K - $100K	$50K - $100K	$5 - $10K	$0 - $5K	$100K - $250K	$0 - $5K	$500K - $750K	$500K - $750K

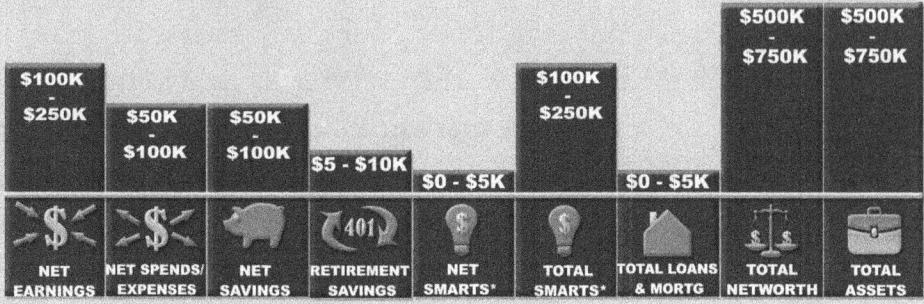

Year	2009
Net Earnings	$100,000 - $250,000
Yearly Net Spending & Investment	$50,000 - $100,000
Yearly Net Savings	$50,000 - $100,000
Yearly Retirement Savings	$5,000 - $10,000
Yearly Smart Savings	$0 - $5,000
Total Smart Savings	$100,000 - $250,000
Total Loans & Mortgages	$0 - $5,000
Total Net Worth	$500,000 - $750,000
Total Assets	$500,000 - $750,000

PERSONAL INSIGHTS:

EXCELLENT
VERY GOOD
GOOD
FAIR
POOR

| HEALTH | FITNESS | SOCIAL | CHARITY | HAPPINESS |

2010

> In the business world, everyone is paid in two coins:
> cash and experience. Take the experience first;
> the cash will come later.
> - Harold Geneen

In this year I started to focus more on charity and how I could give back to my community. I set up regular donations with a couple of my favorite causes. Before you do this, take the time to look into the cause you believe in and see what charities or foundations make the best use of the money they receive. Not all of them put 100% of funds into the cause, and it is worth finding out who allocates how much to each part of their charity. As with anything, donating to a charity should make the most of your money.

At certain point in the year, I felt that I was not doing anything strategically wise with my business pursuits and that I did not have a viable end goal in sight. Though these thoughts were discouraging, they provided me some time to really pause and reflect on what ideas were worth my time and energy into pursuing. While I was going through this thought process, I began to see some more results and felt that my efforts were more fruitful in my mobile application venture. This reevaluation ended up being a great motivating force, as my doubts forced me to learn some more about the market I was trying to enter. I was able to make a more informed decision and enter the new phase of my business with surer footing.

As I see it, time spent thinking about new options, learning new skills, and trying new ideas is never spent in vain. Even if those skills are rarely used or the idea is scrapped, your own learning and growth is the most valuable thing that could have come out of it. The time I spent learning helped make a difference in my day job and allowed me to understand business better. Had I only stayed within the realm of knowledge I was already familiar with, I would not have gained that new understanding that helped me in all areas of my life.

Financial Insights:

This was the year I took a key diversion in my business and went off from the website portal business and took a major leap into mobile application venture. This resulted into additional seed investment into my mobile application development with the launch of my SimplyMobi.com mobile website offering mobile services. You would notice that major part of my spendings is focused on my personal business.

For the second consecutive year, I generated very little smart savings (under $2,000), but made sure I was still building my net savings.

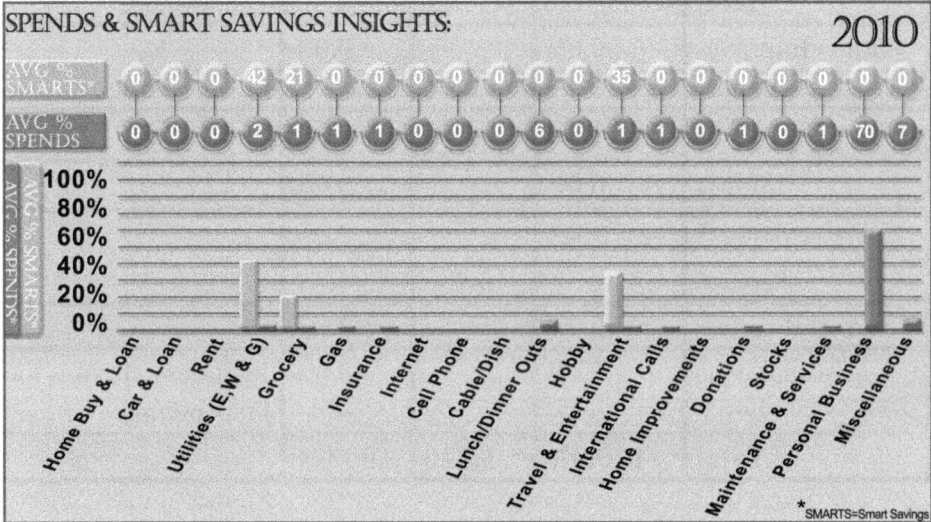

SPENDS & SMART SAVINGS INSIGHTS: 2010

	Home Buy & Loan	Car & Loan	Utilities (E,W & G)	Rent	Grocery	Gas	Insurance	Internet	Cell Phone	Cable/Dish	Lunch/Dinner Outs	Travel & Entertainment	Hobby	International Calls	Home Improvements	Donations	Stocks	Maintenance & Services	Personal Business	Miscellaneous
AVG % SMARTS*	0	0	0	42	21	0	0	0	0	0	0	0	35	0	0	0	0	0	0	0
AVG % SPENDS	0	0	0	2	1	1	1	0	0	0	6	0	1	1	0	1	0	1	70	7

*SMARTS=Smart Savings

Expense Categories	Spending	SmartS $	SmartS %	Notes
Home Buy & Loan	0.0%	-	0.0%	
Car Buy & Loan	0.0%	-	0.0%	
Rent	0.0%	-	0.0%	
Utilities (E,W & G)	2.5%	480	42.9%	+$: Usage conscious
Grocery	1.7%	240	21.4%	+$: Shopping when NOT hungry, NOT thirsty !
Gas	1.1%	-	0.0%	
Insurance	1.4%	-	0.0%	
Internet	0.6%	-	0.0%	
Cell Phone	0.6%	-	0.0%	
Cable/Dish	0.6%	-	0.0%	
Lunch/Dinner Outs	6.5%	-	0.0%	-$: Eating mostly out, no home cooking
Hobby	0.4%	-	0.0%	
Travel & Entertainment	1.4%	400	35.7%	+$: Group Deals, Group Travel
International Calls	1.1%	-	0.0%	
Home Improvements	0.6%	-	0.0%	
Donations	1.8%	-	0.0%	
Stocks	0.0%	-	0.0%	
Maintenance & Services	1.8%	-	0.0%	
Personal Business	70.9%	-	0.0%	
Miscellaneous	7.1%	-	0.0%	Includes expenses for Dependants
Total	100.0%	1,120	100.0%	

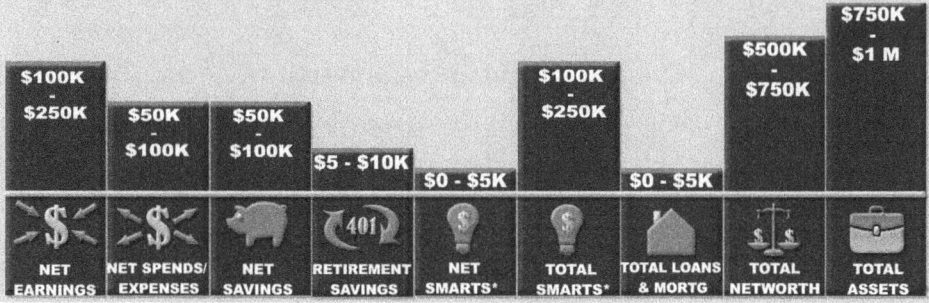

Year	2010
Net Earnings	$100,000 - $250,000
Yearly Net Spending & Investment	$50,000 - $100,000
Yearly Net Savings	$50,000 - $100,000
Yearly Retirement Savings	$5,000 - $10,000
Yearly Smart Savings	$0 - $5,000
Total Smart Savings	$100,000 - $250,000
Total Loans & Mortgages	$0 - $5,000
Total Net Worth	$500,000 - $750,000
Total Assets	$750,000 - $1,000,000

PERSONAL INSIGHTS:

93

2011

> Business opportunities are like buses,
> there's always another one coming.
>
> - Richard Branson

This year arrived very quickly and moved even quicklier for me. Came very fast and started to move very fast for me. I visited India for all of January. Though I was on vacation from my day job, I was working the entire time on my side business as I did not want to fall behind on making progress on something that I could not devote my full attention to anyway.

It was almost going to be my third year of pursuing my business ideas. With the mobile breakthrough this year became the year of my major focus on mobile as I started to see that smart phone mobile platforms were a profitable platform.

This was the first time in over three years that I saw myself breaking even with my business venture. This was a huge milestone for me. At this time, I also made some good fortune from another evening and weekend work given to me by one of my former boss. I was reached out with an opportunity and the requirements suited to my skills. I took that on, even though it was challenging to juggle three jobs at one time (my day job, my business venture and this new opportunity). However, since my technology skills has always been my passion, I was able to enjoy the work I did without feeling overburdened. This third job gave me even more funding to pursue my business effort.

Keep in mind that if you ever need extra cash or need to make some money on the side, there is always someone who does not have—and will need—your skill set. Think about your hobbies or skills that you are passionate about and see if you would benefit from looking at them from a business standpoint (should you need to). For example, one of my friends who loved to cook started a catering service on the weekends. Another friend who is a skilled musician took on students for private lessons in the evenings and on weekends. Another suggestion would be to become a language tutor if you are very proficient in English or another language. Schools sometimes seek translators for foreign students if you know another tongue. Also, seek out freelancing websites and see what is out there. What seems a simple task for you could be quite difficult for someone else—and this could be a chance to forge a mutually beneficial business relationship!

About halfway through the year, I looked at my savings and started to think about doing something with them. Savings interest rates were very low and house values were plummeting, so I felt it was not the best time to let my money just sit in the bank. After a bit of thinking, I decided that I could buy a new house. So I called up the realtor who helped me find my first home and asked her to find me a second house along the same criteria. After a month of searching, I signed papers for a new home that would be ready around March 2012.

Around the same time that I signed for a new house, I got wind of some changes happening at my place of employment. They soon told us that another larger company had bought us and that we would be merging with them. I did not know if this was going to be a negative or positive change for the employees of my company, as acquisitions and mergers are not always transparent in their dealings until everything goes through. After talking it through with my boss, I decided to search for some new career opportunities outside of my company. It made me nervous that I was thinking of leaving my company as soon as I had taken on a second home, and I had to carefully consider if this was a risk worth taking.

Before I moved on, I had a conversation with the new management in which we agreed that I would continue to provide support for the newly merged company through next three months in order to make the transition easier for the company and for me. I realized that this could be a slight setback as it pertained to my personal business plans, but after eight years with the same employer, I felt that I needed the change. The new management proved to have different priorities than the previous management, which only affirmed my decision to move on.

I spent the last few months of the year looking for the right opportunity. I kept thinking about my decision to leave my day job and pursue my own business full time. As I weighed my options, I ultimately decided not to leave my day job just yet, especially because I had a second home mortgage coming on my shoulders now.

Financial Insights:

Keeping my focus on low risk investments, this year my spending was towards investing in my second home and my mobile business. This was the year of hope that I saw with my SimplyMobi.com business venture. This year also marked for lowest in smart savings generated, but at this point I have already managed to generate $100,000 - $250,000 in smart savings through the years till day.

This year I was approaching close to $100,000 in my retirement fund savings. This was a major milestone for me in that area, but I still felt that I should have been saving more per year. Ideally, I had wanted to save an average of $14,000 per year so I would have reached the $150,000 mark by this point. However, I made several attempts to make up the remaining $50,000 by investing in other forms of retirement savings accounts.

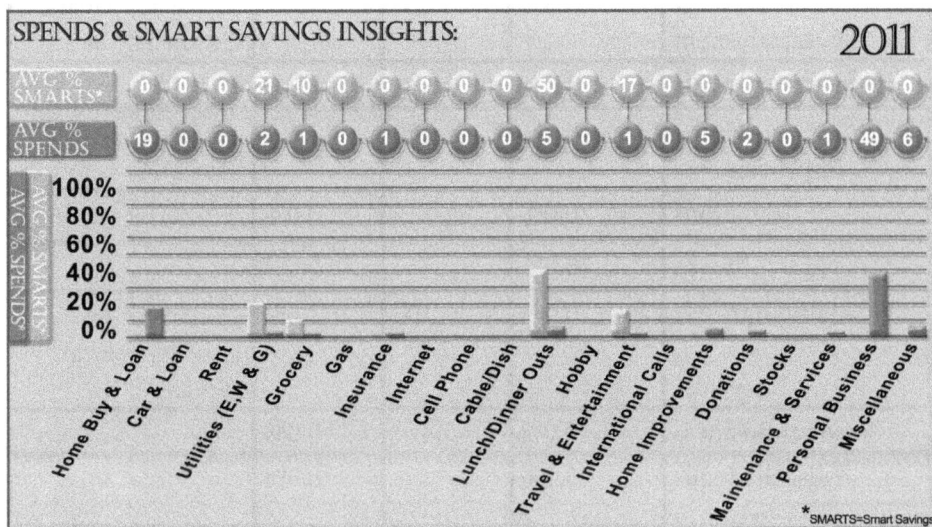

SPENDS & SMART SAVINGS INSIGHTS: 2011

	Home Buy & Loan	Car & Loan	Rent	Utilities (E, W & G)	Grocery	Gas	Insurance	Internet	Cell Phone	Cable/Dish	Lunch/Dinner Outs	Hobby	Travel & Entertainment	International Calls	Home Improvements	Donations	Maintenance & Services	Stocks	Personal Business	Miscellaneous
AVG % SMARTS*	0	0	0	21	10	0	0	0	0	0	50	0	17	0	0	0	0	0	0	0
AVG % SPENDS	19	0	0	2	1	0	1	0	0	0	5	0	1	0	5	2	0	1	49	6

*SMARTS=Smart Savings

Expense Categories	Spending	SmartS $	SmartS %	Notes
Home Buy & Loan	0.0%	-	0.0%	
Car Buy & Loan	35.4%	2,400	21.2%	+$: Employer Loan, Car Model
Rent	26.2%	3,600	31.8%	+$: Roommates/ Shared
Utilities (E,W & G)	4.5%	960	8.5%	+$: Shared, Usage conscious
Grocery	4.1%	600	5.3%	+$: Shared
Gas	5.4%	240	2.1%	+$: Carpool
Insurance	7.9%	-	0.0%	
Internet	0.0%	240	2.1%	+$: In 1999 Dial-up felt sufficient
Cell Phone	0.0%	600	5.3%	+$: Was not necessary yet
Cable/Dish	0.0%	480	4.2%	+$: Local channels sufficed
Lunch/Dinner Outs	1.2%	1,440	12.7%	+$: Cooking home
Hobby	0.0%	-	0.0%	
Travel & Entertainment	4.8%	175	1.5%	+$: Group Deals, Group Travel
International Calls	3.3%	-	0.0%	
Home Improvements	4.1%	300	2.6%	+$: Yard/Garage Sale, DIY
Donations	0.0%	-	0.0%	
Stocks	0.0%	-	0.0%	
Maintenance & Services	0.0%	300	2.6%	+$: Got three years of free car service
Personal Business	0.0%	-	0.0%	
Miscellaneous	3.1%	-	0.0%	
Total	100.0%	11,335	100.0%	

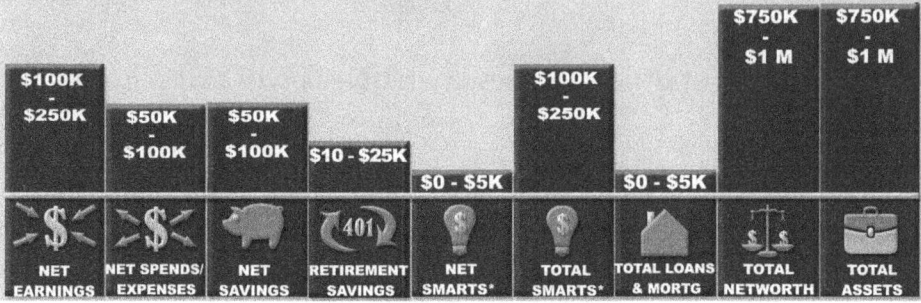

Year	2011
Net Earnings	$100,000 - $250,000
Yearly Net Spending & Investment	$50,000 - $100,000
Yearly Net Savings	$50,000 - $100,000
Yearly Retirement Savings	$10,000 - $25,000
Yearly Smart Savings	$0 - $5,000
Total Smart Savings	$100,000 - $250,000
Total Loans & Mortgages	$0 - $5,000
Total Net Worth	$750,000 - $1,000,000
Total Assets	$750,000 - $1,000,000

PERSONAL INSIGHTS:

99

2012

Beware of little expenses; a small leak will sink a great ship.
- Benjamin Franklin

It felt like 2012 arrived just as I was settling into 2011. The new year greeted me in an alarming fashion—a $2,000 charge that might have been preventable if not for my carelessness and laziness.

One of the toilets flush in my house had started leaking a little bit once in a while. It was a small leak, just enough to wet the tiles around the toilet and dry within an hour. I did not pay much mind to it and told myself that I would get around to fixing it as soon as I had some free time. Unfortunately, I did not have very much free time! What I was not considering was that there was damage occurring underneath the tiles that I could not see. After a month of noticing the leak, I was sitting downstairs and looked up to notice a bulging three-foot long crack in the ceiling. Though at first I was unsure of the cause, I realized that it was right under the upstairs bathroom with the leaky toilet flush. I called a plumber and he confirmed that the leak was indeed the cause. I thought the water from the leak was just drying; the plumber noted that it was actually soaking into the flooring and into the living room ceiling.

Fixing the leak only set me back $120. Fixing the crack in the ceiling and tending to the drywall were going to cost me a substantial amount more. Luckily, the plumber was also experienced in working with drywall and offered to fix my ceiling as well for the sum of $700.

After that, I made the decision to have the house repainted and have all the small cracks covered—after eight years of living there, it could use some freshening up. This latter task—fixing the wall and repainting the house—came out to $1,900 total and took about four days, but the end result made me quite happy.

In mid February, I went ahead and took a new job at a company that was more in line with my skills and interests. Though my commute increased considerably, it was an interesting change and a worthy challenge.

During the transition to my new job, the construction on my second home was coming to completion. However, I found out that the deck—which was agreed upon in verbal discussions—was not built. When I called the builders, they said that the deck was never a part of the deal. I took matters to customer service when I found an email exchange from the previous year in which the deck was discussed. Eventually, I was able to convince them to build the deck based on our email exchange. From this conflict I learned to never agree to sign a deal unless all components are put on paper.

Here I was in April ready to close on my second home. It was ready and inspected. Even up until this date I had not decided if I was going to move into this new home or if I would rent it and continue living in my first home. I was also trying to determine how much of a down payment I should make and which mortgage company I should work with. The builder's company told me that I would get a very good discount towards my closing costs if I opted to go with their mortgage company. This was a different case then what I faced during my first home buying experience. After some consideration, I decided to make the highest down payment possible for me at that time. This approach encouraged me to opt for the builder's preferred mortgage company and to take advantage of closing cost discounts.

I managed to secure a 2.25% mortgage rate when I opted for a 5-year ARM. This time I set an aggressive goal for myself to pay off my second home mortgage in less than five years. I also opted for automated mortgage payment and opted for additional principal deduction to help reduce the interest paid. One can always argue if this was the right thing to do as one can get tax benefits on the mortgage interest (as it it non-taxable). However, I believe that in the long run it is more beneficial to pay off your mortgage instead of holding it to get tax benefits. Below I have some more tips about mortgage that I feel are worth sharing.

Mortgage Tips

I made sure to keep my mortgage within 25-30% of my earnings. This is the primary reason I did not opt for a single family home or larger townhome—it would have forced me to go beyond my 25-30% limit. Avoid going for a second mortgage option as that would drain most of your earnings, put you on a tight budget, and leave almost no room for savings. If you are buying a new home, then you might not have to factor in additional maintenance costs that an older home might incur, even in the first year of your ownership. If you can, take advantage of 5/7 years ARM it will give you the benefit of a lower interest rate. The key to planning an aggressive payoff in 5 years is to go for an ARM as that will help you save probably 2% or more on interest. Try your best to put as much into the down payment as possible while still keeping enough in the bank for the next six months of payments (keep in mind you will have other expenses). As you start planning to buy your home, keep a very close eye on your credit score as well. The better your score, the better the deals you will be able to negotiate. Saving 2% or 3% on interest adds up to big savings in the long term!

Soon I completed on all the closing formalities for the second home. I decided to stay in my old home and rent this new one. I asked my realtor to find a good tenant for me, an exercise that took nearly two months. I was very happy and relieved to sign the rental papers and see the home finally occupied as I had been getting anxious after a month of advertising. According to my realtor, it takes an average of two months to find a renter, so we were right on target.

While things were going fine with my new job , there was a need for me to be flexible and do some traveling. However, I was not ready for travel given I had my mother staying with me and she was not in good health. So I decided to take a different path to show my worth by choosing a new opportunity that was closer to my house and involved no travel. Although it was a great job, there were circumstances that did not allow me to remain in the position for much longer. I reached out to several people for new opportunities and was fortunate to have my ex-boss present a job offer to me. I aggressively pursued this offer and went in for a couple of interviews, after which I was hired. I resigned from my former employer (my shortest stint at a company ever) and began calling my ex-boss simply "boss" again in June. .

I filled up my second "Smart Savings Jar" around early December. At this point I took another look at my savings and my emergency funds. After doing some math, I decided to pay off the entire mortgage of my second home, too.

On December 20, I received a letter from my mortgage company informing me that I had paid off everything. It was a great moment in my life—with this last payment, the house was mine! The home appraisal value went up by nearly $40,000 and I came to the realization that I had a net worth over one million dollars. Eighteen years into my professional career and 14 years into my stay in the US, I was finally free of the burden of a mortgage which gave me more financial freedom than I had ever had before.

Now given that I made the complete mortgage payment, I was able to achieve smart savings of over $125,000. Wonder how? Here is my simple math:

Loan Amount	Loan Rate	Loan Term	SmartS	Notes
$300,000	2.25%	30 years	$125,000+	$+: No Home Mortgage Interest $s payments savings

Running through the amortization calculator, at the end of 360 months, I would have paid more than $125,000 in interest if I had kept all my savings in bank and not used it for paying off on my purchase.

At this point, I reached out my home insurance company to make sure I had everything switched over for payment to me and added as much extended coverage as possible. Be very particular about your home insurance coverage and even auto insurance coverage. I would recommend doing comparisons amongs several different insurance companies to make sure you are not missing out on anything, coverage or pricewise. Another thing is to make sure you have a good home warranty as your home and appliances will last beyond the regular warranty provided by manufacturers.

While I have been thinking along creating a difference since several years, one thought came to me probably around July 2012, this thought was around how I can share my journey with everyone. Key reason this thought started coming to my mind as I felt we in the USA really need to focus towards savings. With that thought in mind, I felt I did a very decent job with my savings while at the same time I did enjoy my life too. With that in mind, I started writing this book as and when I got the chance in the evenings and weekends. I am really hoping that my efforts really bring value to lots of individuals who have been dreaming of being a millionaire or live a life of financial freedom. I believe it could be of great value for common man within USA and all around the world in general!

Financial Insights :

They say nothing is permanent but change. For me the biggest change was to change jobs after almost being at my employer for over 8 years. Change was primarily driver of my employer company getting acquired by another company that resulted into planned layoffs. I volunteered to move on working out a mutual win-win deal only after making sure I will be able to find something compatible elsewhere. This helped me with a monetary lift. I leveraged all my savings from past years plus the voluntary compensative package to payoff all my mortgage of my 2nd home. This marked an year of another major financial freedom from paying mortgage payments.

This is the year I crossed the million-dollar mark not only with my total assets, but also with total net worth. Additionally, this year I crossed the half-million dollar mark in my smarts savings after 14 years of using this system. I think that if I had not stayed focused on my smart savings model, I would not have been able to call myself a millionaire by the end of this year!

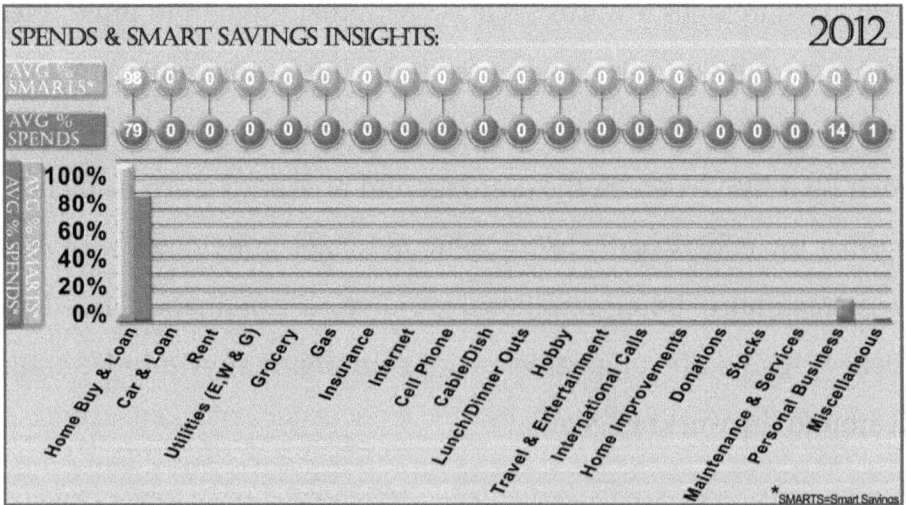

SPENDS & SMART SAVINGS INSIGHTS: 2012

AVG % SMARTS*	98	0	0	0	0	0	0	0	0	0	0	0	0	0	0	0	0	0	0	0	0
AVG % SPENDS	79	0	0	0	0	0	0	0	0	0	0	0	0	0	0	0	0	0	0	14	1

*SMARTS=Smart Savings

Expense Categories	Spending	SmartS $	SmartS %	Notes
Home Buy & Loan	79.4%	119,000	98.6%	+$: Low Mortgage rate, Pay-off New Home Mortgage
Car Buy & Loan	0.0%	-	0.0%	
Rent	0.0%	-	0.0%	
Utilities (E,W & G)	0.5%	480	0.5%	+$: Usage conscious
Grocery	0.4%	240	0.4%	+$: Shopping when NOT hungry, NOT thirsty !
Gas	0.2%		0.0%	
Insurance	0.3%	-	0.0%	
Internet	0.1%	-	0.0%	
Cell Phone	0.1%	-	0.0%	
Cable/Dish	0.1%	-	0.0%	
Lunch/Dinner Outs	0.1%	-	0.0%	-$: Eating mostly out, no home cooking
Hobby	0.1%	-	0.0%	
Travel & Entertainment	0.3%	400	0.4%	+$: Group Deals, Group Travel
International Calls	0.2%	-	0.0%	
Home Improvements	0.7%	-	0.0%	
Donations	0.6%	-	0.0%	
Stocks	0.0%	-	0.0%	
Maintenance & Services	0.4%	-	0.0%	
Personal Business	14.7%	-	0.0%	
Miscellaneous	1.8%	-	0.0%	Includes expenses for Dependants
Total	**100.0%**	**121,272**	**100.0%**	

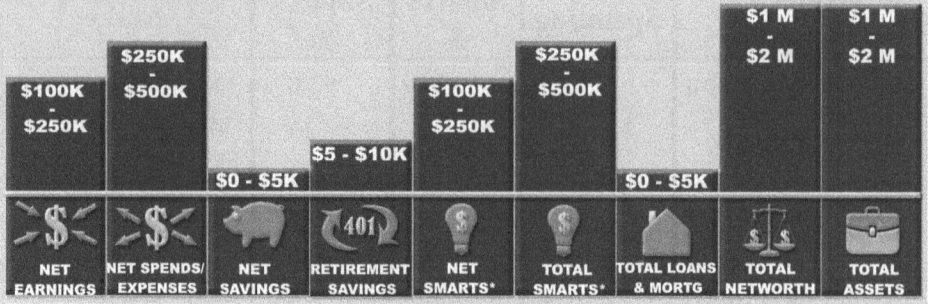

Year	2012
Net Earnings	$100,000 - $250,000
Yearly Net Spending & Investment	$250,000 - $500,000
Yearly Net Savings	$0 - $5,000
Yearly Retirement Savings	$5,000 - $10,000
Yearly Smart Savings	$100,000 - $250,000
Total Smart Savings	$250,000 - $500,000
Total Loans & Mortgages	$0 - $5,000
Total Net Worth	$1,000,000 - $2,000,000
Total Assets	$1,000,000 - $2,000,000

PERSONAL INSIGHTS:

2013

> **Investing is laying out money today to**
> **receive more money tomorrow.**
>
> - Warren Buffett

I finally reached the million-dollar mark at the end of 2012, 29 days away from my 14th anniversary of my arrival to the US (I landed on January 29, 1999). Though I do not have any regrets about my journey or the way things went, I would have liked to try some things differently. I would have educated myself about stocks earlier on and learned how to invest properly. I would have done more thorough research on starting a business instead of diving headfirst. Instead of paying off my second home, I might have used that money to invest in another property. But none of these things are regrets for me, as I learned invaluable lessons in money management and financial decision making that I would not have learned otherwise. One other thing I wish I had done different was to invest in India especially in the real estate market of India.

This year I repeated a mistake that incurred more charges for me—I suffered from kidney stones for the second time. Even though I went under a procedure to remove them in 2008, I did not commit to drinking enough water and saw their return. This resulted in unexpected expenses beyond what my medical coverage, even though it was easily preventable. The key message here is that health is wealth! A healthy lifestyle is a proactive lifestyle that requires giving your body and mind attention—especially when it comes to issues that are preventable and have a tendency to return. Additionally, many employer insurance plans provide benefits and perks for healthy employees—be mindful of these and take advantage of them when you can.

Lifestyle Insights:

This time let me summarize the importance of the 80-20 rule as it pertains to everyday life and social situations, and how I used it to maximize my time. At one point in time, my social circle was very wide. With the passage of time and with the diverging life paths we chose, it became harder and harder to keep up with everyone in that circle. I slowly pulled myself away from the wider circle and chose to focus my social activities and leisure time with my closest friends and family, as they influenced me and my time more than the rest of the circle. There are still instances in which I will find myself at a gathering that is larger than usual or an event for someone outside of my immediate circle, just so I do not become completely disconnected. My time, however, is spent mainly with my inner circle of friends and family.

With loans, mortgages, and investments, I leveraged the 80-20 rule by making sure that I gave prioritiy to the 20% of the loans that comprised 80% of total expenses. I made sure to pay them off as fast as I could and factored them into my purchasing behavior. I also made sure that the 20% of my investments (homes, car, furniture) that account for 80% of my assets were not going beyond my power to quickly pay-off the loans and mortgage. This strategic thinking was key in reaching my goals.

On the work front, I did my best to prioritize by first focusing on the 20% of work that in theory accounts for 80% of value or results that I needed. Once those are knocked down then I would attack the rest while making sure I filter out the noise and distractions that come throughout the day via email and other such quick notices.

As my journey in this book wraps up, I am still in learning more and more about finances and the balance of life and work. Financial freedom is not a goal, but rather a continuing journey. I have achieved a milestone in my life, but I am still working to achieve the next one, and am still passionate about pursuing my own personal business interests, creative ways to invest my money, and now more than ever, ways to give back to my community. Charity was a neglected focus through much of my life. It was always at the back of my mind, but never something that received much time, attention, or contributions from me. As I have settled down, I have become more and more concerned with how I can give back to the world, how I can help mankind and nature, and how I can leave a positive impact. I researched several charities and nonprofits and found a couple that truly touched me, and have made it a priority to give to these organizations as much as I can.

Before I move to the last section of the book, let me lay out a quick visual summary of my fiscal journey: my spending, investments, personal and monetary growth from 1999 through 2012.

Over 14 years, I generated a total of $400,000 - $500,000 in smart savings year over year. This undoubtedly helped me achieve the million dollar mark a few years earlier than if I had not been applying the concept to my savings. Staying in line with the 80-20 rule that 80% of effects can be attributed to 20% of causes, the majority of my smart savings were derived from the auto loans, home mortgages, shared accommodations, and group deals. I made sure that my net expenses always stayed below my net earnings and, more importantly, that my net expenses were mostly below the 50% mark of my net earnings.

Aside from smart savings, I did not let my actual savings sit idly, but invested them into building my assets and reducing my loans/mortgages whenever I could. Though I never let my savings account get low on a regular basis, at a few points I used all of it to invest in my assets or pay off a loan in one go in a calculated effort to reduce interest. Even when I did this, I made sure that my net spending was still lower than my net earnings.

Additionally, I never fell into the habit of making large impulse purchases such as extravagant cars or luxurious home furnishings. I was able to generate smart savings by always going for what I needed instead of what I wanted. On the same note, I knew that I needed to save for retirement as much as possible, so I tried saving on an average anything between $10,000-$15,000 per year for that.

On personal level, my contributions to charity were fairly poor in the first few years after I moved to the US, but as I started to gain some ground after achieving a certain level of financial freedom, I made sure to increase my contributions and become more involved in the charities I truly cared about. Remember that happiness is not just financial freedom, but sharing your freedom with those who are not as fortunate.

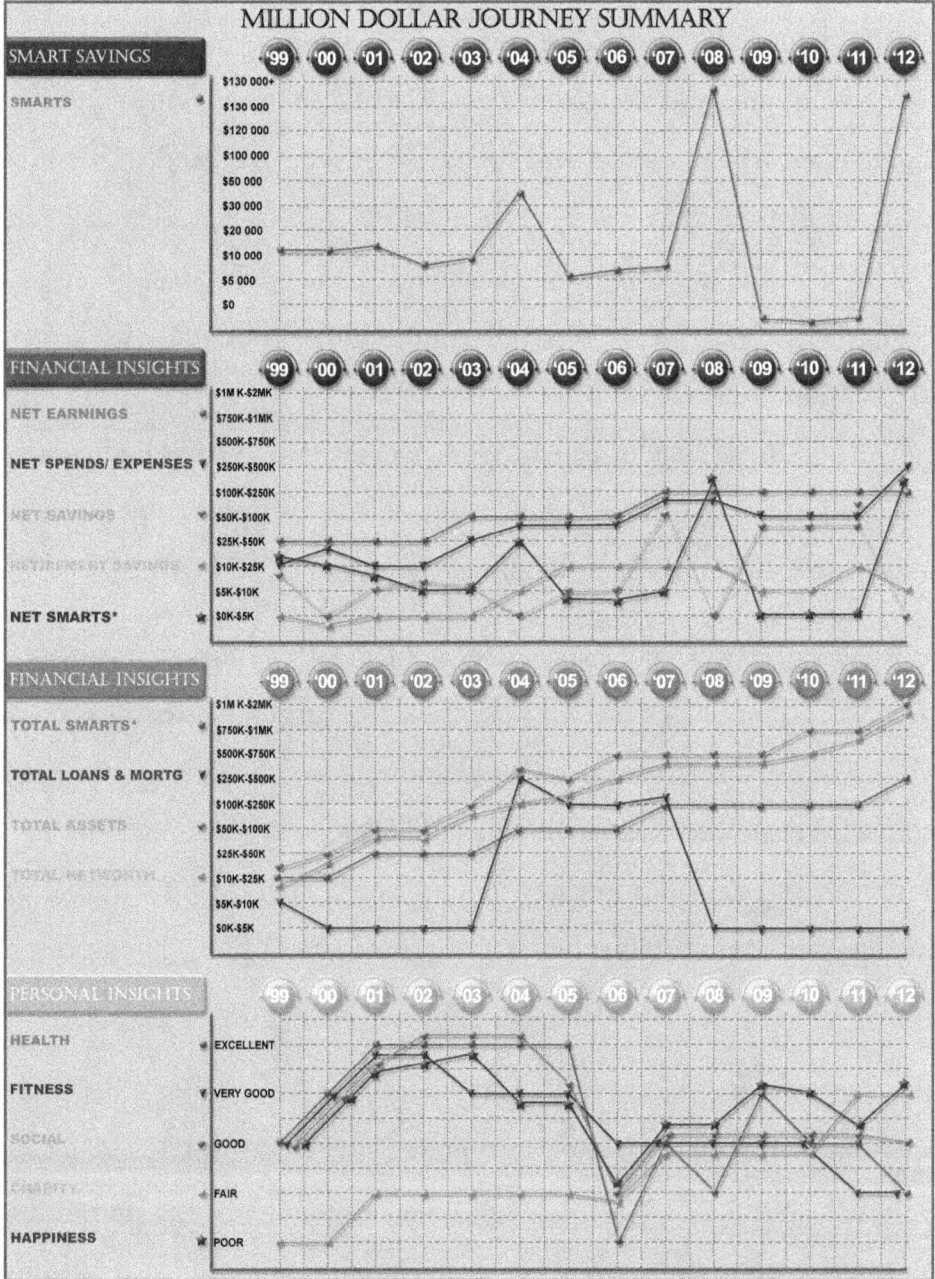

MILLION DOLLAR JOURNEY SUMMARY

FINALLY – ARE YOU READY?

As I finish this book, I want to leave you with some thoughts and words of encouragement. Are you ready to commit yourself to saving? Time is money, and the sooner you act, the more of both you save. Remember, to get started and to stay involved, you need to identify your motivation that will keep you going. Do not just identify your "commit force" in your head—make a list that you can look at and review whenever you see yourself losing sight of your goal. Just as you are passionate about your hobbies, your family, your work, make saving and financial freedom a passion as well. Passion brings dedication. Dedication brings focus. Focus brings vision. Vision brings success. With success everything else follows.

Along the way, make sure to set mini goals for yourself. With each goal you accomplish, you will get a feeling of fulfillment that will push you towards your larger goal. On that note, stop questioning your larger goal. Set it, and then focus on your smaller goals along the way. Financial freedom is a journey, not an exam. There is no winning or losing—set your own standards and grow beyond them as you reach them.

On a more practical note, make wise spending a habit. Keep your spending within your means, and not a cent past. Think twice before you make purchases. Give yourself time before making big purchases. Research your options, even if it means looking something up on your phone before you walk to the cash register. Try different saving models and see what works for you. When you find a system that is suited to your lifestyle, replicate it in every area of your financial life. Additionally, seek a mentor—find someone whose life and financial model you admire and go to them for advice when you need it.

Most importantly, remember that there is no good time to start. There is no difficult time to start. You will always have temptations and you will always have bills. You can rationalize as much as you want, but realize that you are wasting time by doing so. There is only one answer to the question I posed above: yes, you are ready! This is as ready as you will ever be. The best time to start saving is NOW!

Stay connected with millionomics network by visiting

Millionomics.NET

BEHIND THE CURTAIN

I thought it would be interesting for me to share my journey of how I came to write and self-publish this book.

First Round

After I was inspired to start writing this book, my first step was to open a new Microsoft Excel spreadsheet. Yes, over a Word document, I started an Excel sheet because I am a data guy and love to structure everything first. I started with three columns in Excel—one for the year, the second for giving a name to the topic that I wanted to address, and the third one for me to adding notes and a brief anecdote.

The next step was for me to start on writing down the topics I wanted to share. Initially, I started from 1999 to list them down. I saw that it was pretty difficult to recall things from 14 years back! But as I started to write the topics down, more and more details came back to me. I felt I was going in an organized fashion by approaching this year by year. But within a few days of me writing down topics as I remembered, I realized that I had gone off track. However, this ended up being beneficial in the long term.

I found that things started to come to me from different years. As they came to mind, I would immediately make a note of that topic with a slight description in my Excel under its respective year. Within I would say a couple of weeks, I had almost 100 rows created with an average of six to seven topics for almost each year. Additionally, there was a brief description on the topics to help me come back and expand it. Now, remember that I am not doing this full time. I have a day job and I have a second night/weekend job, too (which has now become more my passion than anything else). Even though this process was time consuming, I made sure it did not affect my day to day life or my performance at my day job.

I came to a point with my Excel spreadsheet that I had enough topics and descriptions. It was time to take a deeper dive into each topic and start writing the real content . By the time I expanded on a couple of topics, I became bit uncomfortable navigating around in Excel to read or edit the content. Though Excel really helped me get started and put structure around my writing, it was time to move this phase into a word processing tool. Once I migrated the content to Microsoft Word from Excel, I felt like I had an entire playground open just for me. I felt more relaxed in writing and was ready to go.

It took almost six or seven weeks to fully expand on each topic. I never gave a second thought about whether or not I should mention something, but just kept writing everything and anything that came to my mind. One thing I learned during the process was that I just cannot set myself a certain fixed hours of window dedicated to writing. I just have to find the opportunity whenever I can and write. Here I was still in the raw draft stage of writing; editing, refining, and finishing is going to be the next step. At the start, it is just important that you write, write and just write, staying on the topic!

It was over two months already and I had put about 80 hours into writing and planning my work. One of the most interesting things that happened was that the deeper and deeper I went into the details of writing, the more thoughts I would have come to me at random times during the day. I could be walking or in the bathroom or trying to sleep or, at times, even trying to meditate and these thoughts would seep into my head. As thoughts and ideas came to me on what I should add further to my book or how I should organize it better, I started to get overwhelmed. It might take a day for me to even remember all of them. So at this time, I would immediately make notes on my cell phone or iPad and send into myself. The key point is, just so that I did not lose any of my thoughts or ideas, I started making notes of them as soon as they came to me. Taking mental notes was not that effective for me!

The Pause

In October, I felt I was around 30-35% done with the overall writing. I had put maybe say around 100 hours of my time in the form of real writing, thinking, reading and more. Right around this time, the distractions kicked in. For some reason my "commit force" were not that strong to divert back or stop the diversions. I started to notice that I found reasons to keep myself busy enough with other things that I had no time to continue on my writing. I would open my book almost every day but would not even make an attempt to complete a paragraph. This continued for almost two or three weeks. Why was my "commit force" not strong enough for me to push through? I started to feel that I did not have the patience to write and there was no way I could write enough to accomplish a book worth of quality, focused content. I started to feel that it was getting difficult for me to create a balance between my day and night job with the added project as well.

I realized that I need to take a break and decompress. I decided to not think or touch the topic of writing for at least the next two weeks. Instead, I would just stay focused on my day job and a bit of my night job to keep operations running. I felt relaxed and became rejuvenated. So after two weeks, I decided to again open up the book and continue my writing. But this time I decided to worry less about hard dates and not look at it like another job. I told myself to stop focusing on how many pages I had written and instead focus on the writing and the content

Second Round to Launch

Here I was in my second round of writing with my new guidelines in mind. I spent my entire long Thanksgiving weekend in November mostly dedicated to writing. Believe it or not, within those three or four days, I accomplished almost another 20-30% of writing. So what I accomplished in the initial three months of writing, I also accomplished in these four days!

After Thanksgiving weekend, I did my best to keep up with the momentum. During the weekdays, I would find even a half hour at night to write more. By the end of December 2012, I was finally done with my first draft. I was excited and delighted that I really completed my manuscript, but I knew I was only done with the first phase and had many more steps to complete. I also started reading and researching about book writing and publishing on the Internet to get some ideas on what I should be focusing on. After a bit of reading online, I knew that I had to go through my draft several times and edit it. I had several friends read the book to give me their feedback and also hired a couple of editors to read through with a critical eye and make changes.

Because I was a first-time author without a book deal, I knew that self-publishing an eBook was my best option. This allows distrubution through Amazon's Kindle Direct Publishing (for use with their Kindle e-reader), Apple's iBookstore (for use on iPads and iPhones), Google Play (for use on Andriod devices), Barnes & Noble (for use on the NOOK e-reader), and Canada's Indigo Bookstores (for use on their Kobo e-reader). In the course of my research, I also found out that there are several other online channels for selling books directly to the consumer by means of website services like E-junkie, ClickBank, and Gumroad.

However, I wanted to see a printed version of my book, too. I came across two worthy options. The first was Amazon's Createspace and the second was Lulu.

Around mid-January I decided to read my draft all over again to fill in gaps and information that I felt would be relevant. As I started reading my draft, I felt that there was a need to show some hard financial numbers and relevant insights alongside the personal insights.

Given I am a fan of infographics, I decided I should probably add some infographics to my work. I came up with a sketch of what I wanted the infographics to look like and assigned the task to a hired infographic designer. It took the person one week to deliver back all the infographics based on the mock-ups I shared with him.

I already knew that a few of friends would love the concept and appreciate it and expected others to be more critical. I also knew that I needed both perspectives to improve further. With that said, take criticism positively and improve upon the feedback instead of being disappointed and disheartened. I was lucky to have several friends who were open to reading my draft and found the time to read thoroughly and provide good feedback. At this point, I sent the book out for copyediting and general editing.

Here I am with the publishing of my first book! I truly hope that my honest advice and efforts are able to bring value to each of my readers' lives. My first launch is going to be in the form of an ebook, but if all goes well, then I would like to see this take the form of a physical book, an audio book, and maybe even a mobile app.

REFERENCE GUIDE
Spending Tips & Statistics

Here are some statistics to get you thinking about your spending habits.

- Buying branded or designer products usually costs higher almost 20-60% more in grocery stores. Based on my experience, sticking to house brands can yield yearly savings of $2,000 - $5,000.

- Instead of eating out, try to bring your lunch to the office for at least four days. With this method I saved $150-$200 per month, which yields a yearly savings of $1,500 - $2,500.

- Maintain presence of mind and avoid doing multiple tasks when driving. Common mistakes cause unforeseen expenses (such as hitting your car while backing out of the garage). Also, learn basic car maintenance, such as checking oil and fluids so you know when to go and get it serviced (and not more than you need)

- If it suits your lifestyle, adopt the sharing model where possible. Share an accommodation if you are a single. Share a ride to work. Take group vacations.

- Keep putting in as much added principal as you can to your house mortgage and auto loan. Yearly Savings: $5,000 - $20,000

- Whenever you see you are building up debt, stay on top by cutting down on all possible expenses that are not necessities.

- Be loyal to some of the stores where you get things you need and if you do that do make sure to become their member so you get member deals/discounts or take advantage of loyalty programs.

- Raising deductibles on various insurances helped me generate savings of up to 30%, which added up to yearly savings of $200 - $400.

- Get your gas filled up at a gas station in your commute that is priced lowest. You can almost save up to $5 for each time you get the tank full. There are apps and websites to help you find the prices of all nearby gas stations. Based on my personal experience, this adds up to yearly savings of $200 - $300.

- Try to keep three or four months' salary in a separate savings account as "emergency cash." I pretended it was not there when making spending decisions. Whenever I did tap into it (as I did for a few major expenses), I made sure to prioritize filling it back up as soon as I could.

Packing Tips

- Important Documents

  * Passport

  * Green Card (especially if traveling abroad)

  * Boarding passes

- Travel Essentials

  * Camera

  * Shaving kit

  * Socks

  * Underwear

  * Pajamas

  * Comfortable shoes

  * Medications

  * Toothbrush

  * Toothpaste

  * Deodorant

  * One set of nicer clothes

  * Chargers

  * Travel umbrella

  * Weather appropriate outerwear

Credit Score Tips

- Enable online bill payment

- Set up autopayment for bills and certain nonnegotiable monthly payments (utilities, subscriptions, etc.)

- Avoid opening too many credit cards—try to keep it around three.

- Avoid getting into any payment disputes that can land into the laps of collection bureaus

- Remember, no credit is bad credit! Use credit cards to leverage your credit score, not to harm it.

- Pay a little bit more than the amount billed

Stores and Websites

Here are some of the stores and websites that I frequent for my purchases, due to their consistent quality and pricing.

Stores:

- Walmart for all my basic home necessities

- Giant for regular grocery shopping

- Lotte Plaza for produce and international foods

- Best Buy for electronics

- IKEA for all home decoration and furniture

- Costco for bulk purchases

- Kohls for clothing

Online Stores:

- Amazon.com for anything you can imagine—worth coming here to compare prices and to do product research

- Zappos.com for shoes

- Ebay.com for variety of my needs

Charities:

- American Leprosy Missions (http://www.leprosy.org)

- National Multiple Sclerosis Society (http://www.nationalmsso-ciety.org)

GLOSSARY

4

401K – Retirement or pension plan, often organized through one's work.

A

Amortization – amortization is the process by which loan principal decreases over the life of a loan. With each payment, a portion of it is applied towards reducing the principal, and another portion is applied towards paying the interest on the loan.

ARM (Adjustable Rate Mortgage) – Also called a Variable Rate Mortgage. The interest rate varies based on many factors and can be changed at the lender's discretion.

B

Bonds – a debt security issued by certain institutions such as companies and governments. A bond entitles the holder to repayment of the principal sum, plus interest. Bonds are issued to investors in a marketplace when an institution wishes to borrow money. Bonds have a fixed lifetime, usually a number of years;

C

"Commit Force" – Your internal force which allows you to commit to a certain activity. Some may call it will power others may call it passion but I call it "commit force" as I believe it's a combination of both that brings a level of commitment within us.

Compound interest – arises when interest is added to the principal, so that, from that moment on, the interest that has been added also earns interest. This addition of interest to the principal is called compounding. Compound interest may be contrasted with simple interest, where interest is not added to the principal (there is no compounding

Credit report – a negative record of an individual's or company's past borrowing and repaying, including information about late payments and bankruptcy.

Credit score – a numerical expression based on a statistical analysis of a person's credit files, to represent the creditworthiness of that person. A credit score is primarily based on credit report information typically sourced from credit bureaus.

D

Deductibles – a specified amount of money that the insured must pay before an insurance company will pay a claim

Down payment – payment used in the context of the purchase of expensive items such as a car and a house, whereby the payment is the initial upfront portion of the total amount due and it is usually given in cash at the time of finalizing the transaction. A loan or the amount in cash is then required to make the full payment.

In real estate, the asset is used as collateral in order to secure the loan against default. If the borrower fails to repay the loan, the lender is legally entitled to sell the asset and retain a portion of the proceeds sufficient to cover the remaining balance on the loan, including fees and interest added

Down payments for home purchases typically vary between 3.5% and 20% of the purchase price. For car purchases the down payment could be anywhere between 3% and 13%.

F

Fixed Rate Mortgage – A home loan where the monthly payments are equal and cover both the principal and interest over the life of the loan.

H

H1B Visa – A non-immigrant visa which allows foreign workers to be employed temporarily within the US.

Hinglish – Slang for people who speak English with a Hindi accent.

I

Impulse Buying – Making purchases without giving in-depth thought as to the practicality of the buy.

Interest – a fee paid by a borrower of assets to the owner as a form of compensation for the use of the assets. It is most commonly the price paid for the use of borrowed money. When money is borrowed, interest is typically paid to the lender as a percentage of the principal, the amount owed to the lender. The percentage of the principal that is paid as a fee over a certain period of time (typically one month or year) is the interest rate.

L

Life Insurance – Insurance that pays out a sum of money either on the death of the insured person or after a set period.

M

Mutual funds – a type of professionally managed collective investment vehicle that pools money from many investors to purchase securities. While there is no legal definition of the term "mutual fund", it is most commonly applied only to those collective investment vehicles that are regulated and sold to the general public. They are sometimes referred to as "investment companies" or "registered investment companies." Most mutual funds are "open-ended," meaning investors can buy or sell shares of the fund at any time.

P

Points (credit cards) – Bonus rewards given for using a credit card.

Principal – a fixed amount of money that is lent for a fixed amount of time in which it must be paid back as it accrues interest.

R

Retirement Savings – Not included as part of the net earnings

Returns – a profit from an investment

Roth IRA – A type of retirement savings plan

S

Schengen – Primarily the European nations.

Stock market – a public entity (a loose network of economic transactions, not a physical facility or discrete entity) for the trading of company stock (shares) and derivatives at an agreed price; these are securities listed on a stock exchange as well as those only traded privately.

W

Will – a legal document containing instructions as to what should be done with one's money and property after one's death.

Quotes From

B

Benjamin Franklin - one of the founding fathers of United States

C

Charles A. Jaffe - author

H

Harold Geneen - an American Businessman
Horace Greeley - an American newspaper editor

J

Jeff Yeager - author
Joe Moore - an American television personality
John Stuart Mill - British Philosopher

L

Laura D. Adams - personal finance expert

M

M.K. Soni - author

P

Paul Clitheroe - financial advisor and Australian television presenter

R

Richard Branson - an English business magnate and founder of Virgin Group

S

Sarah Beeny - property developer and television presenter
Sidney Carroll - film and television screenwriter

W

Warren Buffett - an American business magnate - investor - and philanthropist

www.ingramcontent.com/pod-product-compliance
Lightning Source LLC
Chambersburg PA
CBHW060044210326
41520CB00009B/1263